SOUL SEARCHING

D0980709

We are moral consultants whether we
want to be or not...
    "co-explorers"

Know where you struggle & why.

SOUL
SEARCHING

Why Psychotherapy
Must Promote Moral
Responsibility

WILLIAM J. DOHERTY, Ph.D.

BASIC
BOOKS

A Member of the Perseus Books Group

Library of Congress Cataloging-in-Publication Data
Doherty, William J. (William Joseph), 1945–
    Soul searching : why psychotherapy must promote moral
responsibility / William J. Doherty
        p.   cm.
    ISBN 0-465-02068-2 (cloth)
    ISBN 0-465-00945-X (paper)
    1. Psychotherapy—Moral and ethical aspects.
2. Psychotherapists—Professional ethics.   3. Interpersonal
relations—Moral and ethical aspects.   4. Responsibility.
5. Ethical therapy.   I. Title.
RC455.2.E8D64   1995
174'.2—dc20   94-44647
                                                    CIP

00 01 02   ◆/RRD 9 8 7 6

For Leah

Contents

Acknowledgments

THIS BOOK WAS WRITTEN AS PART OF AN EXTENDED dialogue with a number of colleagues and friends. I am grateful to my near-namesake Patrick Dougherty, especially for his passion for a just world and for a psychotherapy that promotes community well-being. Patrick was also a perceptive and challenging reader of the manuscript in multiple drafts. Elisabeth Horst gave the manuscript a careful reading, helped me with numerous insightful comments, and shares my vision of a morally sensitive psychotherapy. Sally Maison also gave the book an astute reading, often seeing nuances I had missed.

Away from my local scene in Minnesota, I have been inspired over the years by Robert Bellah, whose writings and professional support have been crucial in the development of this book. David Waters gave early and very helpful feedback, pushing me to be more courageous at times when I was waffling. Dan Dwyer generously gave me the benefit of his expertise in bioethics and in psychotherapy.

I am particularly indebted to the individuals and families who have shared their stories and experiences in therapy with me over the years. What I have learned from them constitutes the heart of the book. To protect their privacy, of course, I have changed identifying information and sometimes used composites of two or more cases.

My agent, Jim Levine, and my editor, Jo Ann Miller, saw this work's potential to reach a larger audience than psychotherapists and provided important assistance in setting the tone and voice for the book.

I thank the Rockefeller Foundation's Bellagio Center in Italy for giving me the opportunity to spend a blissful month finishing the book, immersed in great natural beauty and stimulating community. The book is immeasurably better for the opportunity to reflect, read, and write that the Bellagio Center provided me.

Finally, I want to acknowledge my wife Leah, who read every word and gave me the first feedback on each chapter, whose enthusiasm for the project was very important to me, and who has always supported me and loved me in full measure.

PART I

MORALITY
IN THE PRACTICE OF
PSYCHOTHERAPY

CHAPTER I

Psychotherapy and Moral Responsibility

I N THE LAST DECADE OF A CENTURY THAT HAS WIT-
nessed "the triumph of the therapeutic" in mainstream culture,
psychotherapy in America is facing a crisis of public confidence.[1]
The crisis is not about the perceived benefits of psychotherapy;
more than one-third of all American adults have opted to see a
therapist or counselor at some point in their lives, and polls suggest that most Americans think psychotherapy for personal problems is helpful.[2] Rather, the crisis is over psychotherapy's ability to
speak to the profound social and moral problems of our day. Are
therapists making these problems worse by justifying the contemporary flight from personal responsibility, moral accountability,
and participatory community? This concern is coming from
within the psychotherapy community as well as from without and
is provocatively expressed in the title of a book by the Jungian
therapist James Hillman and his colleague Michael Ventura, *We've
Had a Hundred Years of Psychotherapy—and the World's Getting
Worse.*[3]

Public disenchantment with psychotherapists was evident in
the reaction to the highly publicized Woody Allen–Mia Farrow
child custody proceedings in 1992–93. A prominent issue was

Allen's fitness as a parent, given his secret affair with Farrow's nineteen-year-old daughter. As in most child custody disputes, no one came out unscathed, least of all the therapists who testified as expert witnesses. When questioned about whether they thought Allen was wrong to have had a secret affair with his lover's daughter, who was also the stepsister of his own children, the therapists all demurred from making evaluative judgments. They used language reminiscent of the Watergate hearings: Woody Allen "may have made an error in judgment," the affair was "a mistake given the circumstances," and (my personal favorite) the situation was a reflection of "the postmodern family." Finally, after trying unsuccessfully to get any expert witness to break out of morally neutral therapeutic discourse, the exasperated judge angrily cut one of them off with these words: "I find it extraordinary the words that therapists use who come here … they … say 'bad judgment' or 'lack of judgment.' But isn't there something stronger? You went through the 'postmodern structure of the family' and types of relationships. We're not at the point of sleeping with our children's sisters. What does it mean?"[4]

The expert witnesses were neither fools nor incompetents. Rather, these well-regarded psychologists, psychiatrists, and marriage and family therapists were caught in the web of psychotherapeutic discourse, which has been stripped clean of moral barnacles such as right and wrong, "should," "owe," "ought," responsibility, and obligation. If they had answered the judge's question in moral terms, the expert witnesses would have risked sounding unprofessional and therefore not like experts—a double bind that made me grateful I was not in their position. The incredulous judge, like the numerous newspaper columnists who made similar points, represented the average citizen who believes that moral considerations are still important in understanding and evaluating human behavior.

The American public in the early 1990s then became preoccupied with two criminal trials involving the murder of parents and the mutilation of a spouse—again, the kinds of behavior many people think have something to do with morality. The Menendez brothers of Los Angeles admitted killing their parents after years of what they claimed was physical and sexual abuse by their father. Lorena Bobbitt admitted that she had cut off her husband's penis while he slept and justified her act by pointing to the years of abuse she had suffered from him. The testimony of mental health professionals was key to the hung-jury outcome in the Menendez case and to the acquittal of Lorena Bobbitt (whose husband had been acquitted previously of abuse charges—at least there was symmetry here). On the positive side, these outcomes reflect greater contemporary understanding of the effects of physical and sexual abuse, problems once thought to be rare or only temporarily traumatizing. But many people, as reflected in editorial writing and radio talk show discussions, have expressed concern that the idea of taking personal responsibility for one's actions is vanishing from the public arena, and that therapists have become magicians who can make moral sensibilities vanish under a veil of psychological rhetoric.[5]

The early 1990s also witnessed vehement and unprecedented accusations against therapists for severing family bonds by encouraging clients to recall memories of childhood sexual abuse. The issues here are quite complicated, and mental health professionals themselves are divided on the reliability of adult memory of childhood abuse and on the propriety of some therapists' behavior in eliciting these memories, which sometimes prove to be questionable. My point is that therapists are increasingly portrayed—even in the "Doonesbury" cartoon strip, a bellwether of liberal satire—as at best incompetent and at worst dangerous for encouraging clients to conjure up memories that tear apart their families. Although these characterizations may not be fair or accurate, they are no doubt fueled by the long-standing tendency of media therapists and self-help books to cast parents as villains and oppressors.

This critique of psychotherapy might be dismissed as a by-product of a debased popular culture, except that trenchant commentaries have emerged in sociological and philosophical circles as well. Two of the most prominent philosophers in the world, Alasdair MacIntyre and Jurgen Habermas, have each raised concerns about the impact of the "therapeutic culture" on contemporary mores and morality. Both implicate psychotherapy in the decline of family and community in the Western world. Similar critiques have been made by social scientists and social critics such as Philip Rieff, Robert Bellah, Christopher Lasch, Michael Lerner, and Michael and Lise Wallach.[6]

The erosion of public confidence in psychotherapists comes at a time when therapists are experiencing the worst professional and ethical crisis in the profession's history. The advent of managed mental health care in the U.S. health care system has ended the golden age of psychotherapy—the period from the late 1970s to the early 1990s—during which legions of therapists entered a field that offered plentiful jobs, the promise of good private practice incomes, and a high degree of professional autonomy. Just like medical doctors, therapists came to expect insurance companies to reimburse whatever services the therapist thought were reasonable and necessary. Under managed mental health care, therapists are now expected to cooperate with treatment guidelines developed by third parties, who generally insist on brief treatment focused on a specific, diagnosed mental health problem.

As a result, many therapists feel forced to provide therapy they were not trained for: short-term, problem-focused treatment that does not concern itself with the broader issues of quality of life and human development. The loss of professional autonomy and the increases in malpractice suits and licensing board actions against therapists have generated a profound moral quandary for many therapists, a crisis of integrity in which they feel they must either do right by their clients or do right by third-party payers and licensing boards. The combined economic and ethical squeeze therapists are facing in the 1990s has shaken the field.[7]

Just when therapists need large doses of political support, it has not been forthcoming from citizens who generally appreciate what therapists have done for them personally but who increasingly see therapists in public engaging in psychobabble rather than straight talk about moral responsibility and accountability. Even the columnist Ellen Goodman, normally an advocate of psychological sensitivities, has had enough. Reflecting on the Woody Allen affair, she wrote:

> I rarely side with people who want to put good and evil stickers on every piece of human behavior. . . . The word evil doesn't roll off my tongue either. But there are times . . . when I wonder whether our adoption of Shrink-ese as a second language, the move from religious phrases of judgment to secular words of acceptance, hasn't also produced a moral lobotomy. In the reluctance, the aversion to being judgmental, are we disabled from making any judgments at all?[8]

Therapists are faced with rising public skepticism and the erosion of professional autonomy. We can either howl about being misunderstood and unappreciated or begin a painful reexamination of our contributions to contemporary social problems and to our own predicament. Most of us like to see ourselves as part of the solution to human problems—albeit limited by our own abilities and by external forces—and certainly not as part of the problem. It is easier to see oneself as aiding the casualties of a heartless and fragmented society with easily identified villains: greedy capitalists, self-serving politicians, repressive religious groups. But circling our wagons is an inadequate response to the grave problems of contemporary society.

This book argues that therapists since the time of Freud have overemphasized individual self-interest, giving short shrift to family and community responsibilities. It calls for the inclusion of moral discourse in the practice of psychotherapy and the cultivation in therapists of the virtues and skills needed to be moral con-

a call for moral discourse in psychotherapy

sultants to their clients in a pluralistic and morally opaque world. I argue that issues of moral responsibility and community well-being are always present in therapy, and that carefully balanced attention to these issues can greatly expand the contribution of psychotherapy to the alleviation of human problems. And I propose that therapists' failure to attend to the broader moral and community dimension has left psychotherapy vulnerable to being managed as just one more commodity in the health care marketplace. Morally sterilized psychotherapy has lost whatever moral leverage it could have used against the hegemony of the bottom-line economic decision making practiced by many public officials and managers of health care. With no moral leverage, therapists who advocate maintaining generous mental health insurance benefits sound suspiciously like military defense contractors arguing that reduced military spending will threaten national security.

As in all intellectual endeavors, critique is easier than reconstruction. I owe much of the framework for my social critique of psychotherapy to social scientists who have written about the modern culture of individualism. The most influential, though not the earliest, critique came in 1985 in *Habits of the Heart* by Robert Bellah, Richard Madsen, William Sullivan, Ann Swidler, and Steven Tipton. These authors placed psychotherapy at the center of the growing hegemony of individual self-interest in American society. They argued that most psychotherapists unwittingly promote a form of "expressive individualism," a cousin of "utilitarian individualism"—the idea that if individuals are free to pursue their private economic self-interest, society as a whole will benefit. In expressive individualism, the same logic holds for emotional well-being: we can each focus on ourselves because personal psychological well-being inevitably leads to family and community well-being. At its crudest, expressive individualism is a psychological form of trickle-down economics, in which responsibilities to others are reduced to responsibility to self.

The sociologist Philip Rieff gave a prophetic treatment of these issues in two important books published in the 1960s: *Freud: The Mind of the Moralist* and *The Triumph of the Therapeutic*. Rieff posited that four "character ideals" have successively dominated Western civilization: (1) the Political Man of classical antiquity (I retain Rieff's prefeminist language); (2) the Religious Man (Judaism and Christianity until the Enlightenment); (3) the Economic Man (Enlightenment through the early twentieth century); and now (4) the Psychological Man, whose goal is self-satisfaction and personal insight in order to master "the last enemy—his personality."[9] Beginning with Freud, according to Rieff, "the best spirits of the 20th century have thus expressed their conviction that . . . the new center, which can be held even as communities disintegrate, is the self."[10] As "the therapeutic" increasingly supplants religion as the accepted guide for human conduct, the psychotherapist becomes the de facto moral teacher in contemporary American society.

The problem with the therapist being cast in the role of moral teacher, of course, is that therapists have done their best to stay out of the morality business. A cornerstone of all the mainstream models of psychotherapy since Freud has been the substitution of scientific and clinical ideas for moral ideas.[11] Freud put moral conscience in the superego, a frequently tyrannical, if necessary, bearer of the traditional morality of one's culture. Freud removed morality from the core personality (the ego), and from psychological treatment as well, and therapists have not returned it to either place since. The result has been a reflexive morality of individual self-fulfillment, with relational and community commitments seen as means to the end of personal well-being, to be maintained as long as they work for us and discarded when they do not. Two quotes—the first a frequently quoted Gestalt therapy "prayer" penned by Fritz Perls in the 1960s, and the second from the 1974 best-selling book on midlife transitions by the popular writer Gail Sheehy—illustrate an ideology whose legacy is still with us:

I do my thing, and you do your thing.
I am not in this world to live up to your expectations,
And you are not in this world to live up to mine.
You are you and I am I,
And if by chance we find each other, it's beautiful.
If not, it can't be helped.[12]

You can't take everything with you when you leave on the midlife journey. You are moving away. Away from institutional claims and other people's agenda. Away from external valuations and accreditations, in search of an inner validation. You are moving out of roles and into the self. If I could give everyone a gift for the send-off on this journey, it would be a tent. A tent for tentativeness. The gift of portable roots.... For each of us there is the opportunity to emerge reborn, *authentically* unique, with an enlarged capacity to love ourselves and embrace others.... The delights of self-discovery are always available. Though loved ones move in and out of our lives, the capacity to love remains.[13]

When I read these quotes for the first time in the mid-1970s, I admired their vision and boldness. Now I am appalled at their one-sidedness. I have seen too many parents "move on" from their children, too many spouses discard a marriage when an attractive alternative appeared, and too many individuals avoiding social responsibility under the rubric of "it's not my thing." Widespread reevaluation of the fruits of unfettered self-interest at both the psychosocial and economic levels is under way in the mid-1990s. Some of it takes the form of a rhetoric of return to an earlier era when community traditions marginalized women and minority groups and the pursuit of self-interest (mostly economic) was the privilege of certain white men. But there are many progressive voices of reevaluation, those who appreciate what the ideals of personal freedom and the pursuit of happiness have contributed to the modern world and who see the struggle for freedom and equality as unfinished, who nevertheless believe that the mainstream American cultural values of private gain (both economic and psychological) and communitarian values and responsibilities are badly out of balance.[14]

There are two main reasons for the absence of a moral focus in psychotherapy and for the recent interest in its rebirth. First, for the first six decades of psychotherapy's history, most clients came to therapy with a clear, albeit rigid and unintegrated, sense of moral responsibility. Many people suffered from guilt and inhibitions about feelings and behaviors that were entirely human and not harmful to anyone—masturbation, for example. A married client considering a divorce could be counted on to have internalized the social stigma about divorce and the moral mandate to remain married until death; the therapist might then have helped the client see that personal happiness is indeed a legitimate consideration in the decision to stay or leave, and that traditional notions of commitment do not necessarily require prolonged impairment in both parties in order to maintain a deadly marriage. Psychotherapists saw the oppressiveness of cultural norms dressed up as moral principles and could see themselves as agents of emancipation who deconstructed clients' unexamined but powerful moral codes and helped them to make their own decisions. The moral rules of conventional society, however, could be counted on to provide the scaffolding upon which the client could build a more authentic life.

By the 1990s, however, whatever has served as the moral center of mainstream culture seems not to be holding. Massive cheating in the business world and in military academies, unprecedented levels of crime and violence, shocking reports of physical and sexual abuse in families, widespread abandonment of children by divorced as well as never-married fathers, followed by justifications based on personal entitlement, doing one's own thing, or victimization—these are examples of trends that undermine any concern that contemporary Americans have overlearned a rigidly conventional morality that they must be liberated from by an army of psychotherapists.

James Q. Wilson, a public policy scholar, sums up this point when he describes the context of Freud and other pioneering intellectuals and artists who rejected conventional morality to pursue self-knowledge and self-expression: "[They] could take the product of a strong family life ... [good conduct] ... for granted and get on with the task of liberating individuals from stuffy conventions, myopic religion, and political error."[15] But like contemporary psychotherapists, these avant-garde leaders were borrowing on what Wilson terms the "moral capital" of past decades and centuries. After a hundred years, the moral capital is depleted and therapists no longer need to see themselves primarily as agents of liberation from an ethic of blind self-sacrifice and inauthenticity. At the cultural level, that battle has been largely won, but the fruits of victory are not as sweet as many of us imagined they would be. Even Rollo May, whose early writings were literate and powerful indictments of fulfilling conventional social roles and obligations, has reevaluated the role of psychotherapy in the 1990s:

> We in America have become a society devoted to the individual self. The danger is that psychotherapy becomes a self-concern, fitting ... a new kind of client ... the narcissistic personality.... We have made of therapy a new kind of cult, a method in which we hire someone to act as a guide to our successes and happiness. Rarely does one speak of duty to one's society—almost everyone undergoing therapy is concerned with individual gain, and the psychotherapist is hired to assist in this endeavor.[16]

I don't want to overstate this case, however. Many people still have not gotten the message that they have a legitimate claim on selfhood. Women in particular have been given cultural permission to pursue personal autonomy only in the last few decades, whereas men have had such permission for much longer.[17] These gender differences have important implications for therapists. Some abused women are bound by a Gordian knot of obligation and sometimes distorted religious belief and need a strong message that they have the right to be free of a destructive marriage. There are still many mothers who have learned to put everyone's needs before their own and who must learn to nurture themselves as well as others. But the answer for these individuals is not a therapy that turns them inward to the exclusion of their interpersonal commitments, but a therapy that honors their sense of relational responsibility while helping them to manage both parts of the Golden Rule: Love others as you love yourself.

The second reason for the current upsurge of interest in values and moral issues in psychotherapy stems from the field's loss of innocence beginning in the late 1960s, when established social institutions came under attack. African-American and feminist social scientists and therapists took a hard look at traditional so-called value-free psychotherapy and found rampant biases and distortions.[18] The therapeutic ideal, previously thought to be solidly grounded in science and impartial clinical insight, now looked suspiciously like the creation of white, middle-class North American males. The field could no longer claim value-free, objective neutrality. Simultaneously, the Vietnam War was challenging the idea that psychotherapists need not concern themselves with community and social issues. Robert Jay Lifton, writing in 1983 about his experiences working with survivors of the Vietnam War, asserted that, after Vietnam, "we have . . . outlived the period of ethical neutrality in the professions, the possibility of regarding our work and our place in society as being beyond moral scrutiny."[19]

The critiques inspired by feminists, minority-group therapists, and other social activists in the 1960s and 1970s allowed therapists who were listening to see their work in a larger community context and to be concerned about harming clients through biased attitudes and values. The broad movement for consumer rights

also influenced psychotherapy; professional associations of therapists, newly aware of how therapists could violate clients' rights,
developed ethics codes during this period. Therapist sexual abuse
of clients began to come to light when these ethics codes became
more widely disseminated.

In addition to concern about the erosion of a moral sense of
community and the influence of 1960s and 1970s social movements, more recent influences have affected the reevaluation of
psychotherapy's role. Postmodern theory and a general distrust of
professional expertise in the 1980s and 1990s have generated powerful critiques by psychologists of psychology's role as a perpetra-
tor of selfish individualism and social control by intellectual
elites.[20] Religiously oriented therapists in the 1980s also began seriously to study therapists' moral and religious values and to suggest
that excluding religious issues in psychotherapy might be unnecessary, just as some scholars, such as Stephen Carter, have called for
dismantling the wall of silence between internalized religious
beliefs and public life.[21]

As a result of all these influences, more and more books and articles by psychotherapists on the topic of morality and psychotherapy
are beginning to appear—writings not just about the ethical behavior of therapists but also about moral issues in the lives of clients.[22]
From a variety of quarters, the field of psychotherapy is taking a new
look at itself, and none too soon, given the crisis of confidence that I
believe is taking shape in the larger society.

I wrote this book to take a step beyond critique into reenvisioning
psychotherapy as a moral enterprise. This task, in my view,
requires writing about the heart of therapy—the therapeutic conversation in which shared realities are created and healing occurs.
Thus, case descriptions will be at the heart of the discussion, and
many of the core ideas will be folded into case discussions rather
than laid out didactically, as in this first chapter. Although the
book is written for psychotherapists and other individuals inter-

ested in psychotherapy's role in society, it is not about a particular model of therapy or a particular type of client. I believe that the vacuum of moral discourse holds true for all the dominant models of contemporary psychotherapy, although marriage and family therapy is generally not as biased toward individual self-interest as the more prevalent individual psychotherapy models are. I am interested in how moral discourse can occur in all types of therapy (individual, couples, family, group), in all clinical models of therapy (including psychodynamic, behavioral, cognitive, and family systems), and with clients from a full gamut of ethnic and social class backgrounds.

My own biography and clinical experiences have inevitably informed the ideas delivered in this book. I am a white university professor, psychologist, and family therapist trained in the 1970s. Among the prominent experiences shaping my moral outlook were an Irish Catholic childhood in Philadelphia; the years I spent in a Catholic seminary (the Paulist Fathers), where I studied philosophy and theology; participation in the social justice movements of the late 1960s; my current religious affiliation as a Unitarian-Universalist; a twenty-three-year marriage and two young adult children. Although I have worked with a variety of individuals, couples, and families across ethnic and social class groups, more recently, while I was developing the clinical approaches described in this book, I have been working with mostly white, middle-class, heterosexual clients in my part-time private practice; hence the case descriptions reflect the characteristics of that group. I operate primarily out of a family systems model of therapy, although I use an eclectic blend of therapeutic techniques and work with individuals as well as couples and families. And I have a special interest in therapy with families with a seriously ill or disabled member and in the collaboration among physicians, nurses, and therapists in this enterprise.[23]

I encourage readers to evaluate what I have written in the light of their own experiences and clients and to take what fits, improve on what seems half-accurate, and discard the rest. I am more interested in raising issues than in settling them. But I want to resist forcefully the notion that moral discussion in psychotherapy is appropriate mainly with one client population or another—as if, for example, only educated people have the luxury or the personal resources to contemplate their moral responsibilities, or, equally pernicious, as if the moral lapses of our day are found mainly among poor, inner-city minority people. Why is it that when public officials use the term "moral responsibility" they are generally talking about families on one kind of public assistance and not corporations on another kind of public assistance called tax breaks? There is plenty of moral work to go around.

The first part of the book deals with moral issues in the lives of clients, the second with the moral qualities required in therapists. My intention in both parts is to be illustrative rather than exhaustive. In the first part, I discuss the moral issues of commitment, justice, truthfulness, and community. Chapter 2, on commitment, introduces a framework for moral consultation in psychotherapy that carries through in the subsequent chapters. Chapter 3 discusses the neglected issue of justice or fairness in therapy. Chapter 4, on truthfulness, offers a way to think about the essential linkages between personal authenticity and interpersonal obligations. Chapter 5 describes the ways psychotherapy sometimes contributes to the breakdown of community and ways it can enhance community.

In the second part of the book, I focus on three core therapist virtues: caring, courage, and prudence. My main interest is to establish the relevance of moral qualities or virtues in therapists—beyond their knowledge and technical skill—to their work and training. Caring is the quality that allows them to connect with clients; courage allows them to take risks and face difficult questions; prudence helps them make good decisions in the face of uncertainty.

Throughout the book I use the terms "moral" and "ethical" interchangeably (as they often are in philosophical writing) to refer to issues related to good and bad, right and wrong, obligation and responsibility. My particular focus in this book is on interpersonal morality, on the consequences of our behavior for the welfare of other people—hence the term "moral responsibility" in the title. I use the term "values" with more caution; the range of meanings for this term encompasses truly moral "values," such as respect for the dignity of each person, as well as idiosyncratic, nonmoral values, such as believing in the importance of poetry or athletics. As I have talked with therapists about the ideas in this book, almost everyone has agreed that therapists bring their "values" to therapy, but some become uncomfortable when I speak about therapists' moral beliefs concerning their clients' actions and about explicit discussion of moral issues in therapy that goes beyond "values clarification" (in which everyone's values are presumed equal in moral worth). In my view, the value a father puts on hard work and on maximizing income is not equal to the value of being involved with his son who is feeling abandoned and getting into unhealthy behavior.

The most controversial aspect of this book, then, is apt to be my proposal that therapists at times should consciously influence clients to change their behavior in light of the moral issues involved, as in the case of Bruce, in the second chapter, who considered abandoning his young children after a marital breakup. In my view, we inevitably influence our clients' behavior and moral thinking; therapists have already done it for a century by promoting the morality of self-interest. A crucial issue is how respectful and responsible we are with our influence, and how we respond when clients decline our consultation. This is where the therapist's virtues of caring, courage, and prudence become so important.

A subset of therapists, of course, some better trained in fundamentalist religious traditions than in counseling or psychotherapy, feel free to prescribe moral standards for their clients—for example, by telling abused women to uphold their marriage vows at all costs. I want to distance my version of moral discussion and moral consultation as far as possible from this authoritarian approach. On the other hand, I do not want to yield the moral terrain to those who know too well how others should behave. Not all religiously oriented therapists, it should be emphasized, are moral zealots; many religious therapists and pastoral counselors know how to provide sensitive moral consultation to both those who share their faith orientation and those who do not.

I do not believe that therapists of any type can do good work in the moral domain of therapy without being part of a moral community of colleagues who are struggling with the same issues and part of a broader moral community of diverse individuals and groups. Most case consultation and supervision settings provide little opportunity to explore our moral beliefs and our commitments to community and political well-being. Mainly, we discuss "cases," as if each case were not also a moral passion play being co-created by the client, the therapist, and the community. When we discuss "ethical issues," we are usually speaking about following rules of conduct and avoiding ethical or legal trouble. This narrow focus is partly a matter of having too many difficult cases to discuss clinically and too little time. But more important, therapists have lacked the consciousness that moral conversation pervades psychotherapy, and that it behooves us to become better at what we have been doing unwittingly all along. In the postscript, I make a proposal for creating moral communities among therapists and suggest to psychotherapy consumers what they should look for in a morally sensitive therapist.

It has been said that the two major errors in moral philosophy are thinking you know all the truth and thinking that there is no truth to be known. This is not a book on moral philosophy, but I will weave some philosophical discussion into its chapters. One reason I think psychotherapy is an ideal moral laboratory is that most moral reflection involves not abstract principles but moral sensibilities honed through dialogue with others. Moral issues, in the final analysis, are not so dissimilar from the other life issues addressed in psychotherapy. Therapists help clients to better understand themselves and other people and to be good to themselves and other people, but they traditionally steer clients away from using moral language to describe their experience and their choices, and they refrain almost entirely from using moral language themselves to challenge clients' actions that might harm other people. Not wanting to impose their moral standards, they avoid the topic altogether.

Psychotherapy at its best, however, can be a profoundly humanizing experience that increases our moral capacity.[24] Explicit discussion of moral issues, in everyday life as well as in therapy, occurs not necessarily every day and in every session but at special moments. Using examples such as times of marriage, death, political crisis, and abortion, the sociologist Alan Wolfe describes these moral punctuations of everyday life: "Morality matters most during certain highlighted moments in the life course. . . . These bracketed moments make it possible for people to give account for what they are doing by reflecting on the moral consequences of their actions. The social bond is reinforced through the kinds of symbols and rituals associated with such moments of moral intensity."[25]

To engage in moral consultation, therapists do not have to dictate moral rules or claim to have all the answers. Rather, as Alan Wolfe described the role of the social scientist dealing with morality, the therapist's role is to try "to locate a sense of moral obligation in common sense, ordinary emotions, and everyday life . . . to help individuals discover and apply for themselves the moral rules they already, as social beings, possess."[26] There is nothing esoteric about the "moral rules" discussed in this book: commitment, justice, truthfulness, community, caring, courage, prudence. More than anything else, I appeal to therapists to let these fundamental elements of human experience enter the therapeutic dialogue as legitimate areas of exploration and conviction, rather than avoiding or denigrating them in the name of clinical sophistication.

Psychotherapy has assumed a central symbolic and ritual role in contemporary life. Therapists are privileged to be with people at moments of personal and moral intensity in their lives. In the past, we could naively believe that we were not moral consultants and moral learners in these "bracketed moments," that we could keep our hands clean of the moral residue from clients' decisions, and that we could escape indefinitely the responsibility to define ourselves morally in our professional roles to our clients, our colleagues, and our communities. We can no longer hide behind the wizard's veil of clinical objectivity and moral neutrality. The culture we helped to shape for a hundred years is in crisis, partly because people believed what we told them about the good life. I try to show in this book that psychotherapy has the resources to contribute to the formation of a new cultural ideal in which personal fulfillment will be seen as part of a seamless web of interpersonal and community bonds that nurture us and create obligations we cannot ignore and still be human.

CHAPTER 2

Commitment

I REMEMBER CLEARLY THE MOMENT WHEN I COULD NO longer escape the moral dimension of my work as a therapist. I was meeting with Bruce, a forty-year-old man whose wife, Elaine, had just ended their marriage. He returned from work one day to find that Elaine had tossed his belongings into his car and changed the locks on the house. Overwhelmed and depressed, Bruce came to see me. He told me he couldn't face the thought of going back to his house to pick up his children, three-year-old Karen and six-year-old Scott, for a visit. Even more intolerable was the prospect of returning alone to his small apartment after bringing them back to their mother. Tearfully, he said that he could not face Elaine after what she had done to him, although he still loved her and wanted to salvage their marriage.

The more Bruce talked, the more he began to sprinkle in comments such as, "Maybe the kids would be better off if I just stayed away," and, "I think I might need a complete break. Maybe I should just pack up and move far away." In fact, a few years earlier, Bruce had lost contact with a child he had fathered with a woman he did not marry. I felt dismayed when he talked about abandoning his children, but my training had equipped me with responses like, "What do you need to do for yourself right now to get through this?"

The most challenging statements from the traditional therapy paradigm I could offer a client in a situation like Bruce's were on the order of, "I wonder if you have considered the regret you will feel if you take yourself out of your children's lives," or, "You may not be in a healthy enough frame of mind right now to make long-term decisions." There is nothing wrong with these statements; I used them in my work with Bruce. But I also decided to do something decidedly nontraditional—to challenge him in explicitly moral terms. After listening at length to his pain over the end of his marriage, I gently but forcefully told him I was concerned that his children would be damaged if he abandoned them. His reply—"I'm worried about that too, but what kind of father will I be if I am an emotional wreck?"—gave me an opening to continue on the track of moral discourse.

Throughout the conversation that ensued, I emphasized how important he was to them, even if he didn't think so and even if he was not emotionally at his best. I told him I could certainly understand that he might need a short time-out to collect himself before going back to his old house and facing Elaine again. But he was irreplaceable to his children, and in my judgment, they would carry a lifelong emotional burden if he simply disappeared from their lives. Finally, I reminded him that his children were not responsible for the marital breakup, and that it simply was not fair to make them its casualties. As our conversation unfolded and Bruce pondered his course of action, I made these points not in the form of a lecture but as reflections of my perspective.

I am not the first therapist to respond this way to a client in this kind of situation.[1] Yet I was struck by how little clinical training I had received on the moral issues I was confronting with Bruce— and I had very good teachers. What mainstream theory of psychotherapy could I look to for support? Like many others, I was trained to avoid "shoulding" my clients, to never inflict the language of "ought" on them. I had been socialized into a therapy profession that by the 1970s had developed the firm conviction that "shoulds" entrap people into living life for someone else. The only authentic life was based on heeding the dictates of "I want."

While family therapists receive more training than do individual therapists in considering the perspective of each family member, as a practical matter we also tend all too easily to lose sight of the moral stakeholders who are not present in therapy sessions. Many family therapists are comfortable talking about what clients need and deserve from other family members but are very reluctant to talk about what clients owe other family members in care, commitment, fairness, and honesty. Being a family therapist does not carry immunity to the cultural ideal of expressive individualism.

To some therapists, my pronouncements to Bruce about parental commitment no doubt sound starkly moralistic, but I wanted to make two things very clear to him: I was not neutral on his decision about staying committed to his children, and I was giving priority to his children's long-term needs over his short-term distress. I had established a bond of real trust with Bruce, however; he quickly grasped my point and moved from the question of whether to stay involved to figuring out how to accomplish it. In the end, despite lapses I'll discuss in a moment, he remained a committed father to Karen and Scott and later even reconnected with his child from the previous relationship.

When I describe this case to my colleagues, some point out that I could have obtained the same result—Bruce staying involved with his children—by appealing to his self-interest and emphasizing the guilt and remorse he would have eventually felt if he had abandoned them. I did, in fact, use these appeals, because I think they are valid: parents' relationships with their children can be deeply rewarding; when a parent abandons a child, it is not only the child who is damaged. In dealing with moral decisions, however, I think it is generally a mistake to appeal only to a client's self-interest, even if that appeal "works," because the ethic of personal gain we thus promote erodes the quality of our clients' lives and ultimately the quality of community life.

Expanding the therapeutic conversation beyond the client's self-interest, however, pushes most therapists beyond their training and beyond the resources available in most psychotherapy literature.[2] In most models of therapy, the lingua franca is self-speak: I want, I need, I feel, I think. Even those who also speak "systems" tend to appeal to individuals in terms of personal cost-benefit analysis. The upshot is that even if I, as a therapist, happen to believe that a father has a moral obligation to remain in the lives of his children, I am trained to approach clients only in terms of their self-interest. Being concerned with clients' immediate needs is certainly not an invalid therapeutic concern, but when that becomes our *only* consideration, therapy lacks moral and human depth and therapists end up promoting trickle-down psychological economics.

Stated simply, psychotherapy lacks a conscious moral tradition that can be discussed, debated, and refined. The avoidance of explicit moral considerations has left therapists vulnerable to an implicit moral pedagogy in our work and our writings. Feminists have shown that when therapists have no clearly formulated value system regarding gender relations, they enforce traditional gender norms in therapy, and the pattern holds for other value issues: if you don't have a coherent framework of moral beliefs, you inevitably fall back on good old-fashioned American individualism—which is, in fact, a far more influential cultural legacy than either Mom or apple pie.

At the same time, it is crucial for therapists to distinguish between personal values and moral convictions. Aspiring to a good education is one of my personal values, but I am not invested in getting clients to embrace it. Emotional intimacy, based on mutual self-disclosure, is another of my personal values, but I don't pursue it with clients who let me know that they are quite content to go through life without a lot of what I consider "depth" in their relationships. On the other hand, I consider commitment the moral linchpin of family relationships. It is more than a private, idiosyncratic value that I may or may not choose to promote in therapy. To maintain professional integrity, I believe I must bring this moral value to bear in the therapy I provide and in my teaching and supervision. To treat commitment otherwise is to play into the very style of thinking that initially led Bruce to consider giving up his kids: commitment to one's children is just one of a number of competing personal values to be weighed in a values hierarchy of one's choosing.

Although he decided to remain in his children's lives, Bruce maintained what I consider a "contractual" idea of being a parent: he assumed that his continued investment in his children should be dependent on what the children gave back. This is an especially tempting line of thought for noncustodial fathers who are trying to decide whether to stay involved or "move on." Although Bruce set up regular visits with his children, he tended to expect too much cooperation and too great a return of gratitude on his investment of time and energy. His children's misbehavior and "me first" attitude exasperated him, and he sometimes threatened to cut off visitation if they did not start "showing some respect." Describing his struggles with his children, Bruce spoke the same language he might have used to describe a new love relationship that had hit some shoals: "What is this relationship doing for me that I should stay in it?" The language of family commitment as "covenant"—unbreakable, unilateral, unbrokered parental investment—was completely absent. Bruce did love his children and wanted to remain their father, but he had learned an economic and contractual way of thinking about relationships that was confounding his moral sensibilities.[3]

As might be expected, when Bruce threatened his children with the possibility of ending their visits, they became both more insecure and less cooperative, testing his commitment even more. This pattern changed only after I challenged Bruce's assumption about what kids owe their parents and are capable of giving. I told him that young children do not thank their parents very often. The issue wasn't Karen's and Scott's behavior, but Bruce's ability to offer an unconditional commitment to them. Not until they felt his unswerving emotional investment would Bruce get the cooperation—and love—he was seeking.

After working with Bruce on his commitment as a father, I myself was changed. I began to see moral issues where previously I had seen only clinical issues. I became more aware of how I had been unwittingly promoting a moral agenda of self-interest. For the first time, I was able to translate the insights of social scientists such as Robert Bellah into my everyday work with clients. Take the case of Joe, for example.

Joe had managed to stay committed to his two daughters, then eleven and thirteen, for five years after his divorce. But he was caught up short when his ex-wife remarried. Joe was tortured by the thought that another man was going to raise his children and win their loyalty. He began to distance himself from his daughters and to be more critical of them, even warning them that if he ever learned that they called the new man "Dad," they would pay a terrible, unspecified price. The price, as I came to learn, would be his withdrawal from their lives.

Joe's crisis of parental commitment stemmed from his insecurity about competing with another man in his daughters' lives. He was putting his daughters into a terrible bind: disappoint their mother by rejecting her new husband, or accept the new stepfather and risk losing their father. I worked with Joe and his daughters to help him realize that as their father he was a one-of-a-kind figure in their lives, someone who could not be replaced. After his insecurities became less blinding, I helped him see how damaging it was to his daughters when he let his commitment to them rest on how they felt about someone else. The security of noncustodial, twice-a-month father-child relationships is fragile enough without this impossible burden.

From my moral point of view, Joe was doing wrong by his daughters. It is wrong to manipulate children's loyalties the way he did, and particularly wrong to threaten to use the parental version of a nuclear weapon—abandonment. Joe was not a bad person, but he lacked sufficient moral fortitude to keep his commitment firm. Of course, he also lacked a variety of psychological resources to help him through his crisis. His late father had been inconsistent, his mother had rejected him after his marriage, and his relationships with women were unstable and conflictual. Joe presented plenty to work on clinically. What, then, is the advantage of also describing Joe as lacking moral commitment as a parent? Why not just use clinical, morally neutral language that keeps the therapist out of the moral judgment seat?

Psychological language tends to be long on explanations and short on responsibility. A psychological evaluation of Joe would point out the factors that prevented him from truly committing himself to his children, and the aim of the subsequent therapy, perhaps long-term, would have been to help him get to the point where he could commit himself fully. In the meantime, of course, his children would be harmed just as surely as if he were abusing them. Sometimes it is necessary to do the right thing before understanding why we have been doing the wrong thing.

The moral dimension added urgency to my therapy with Joe and his daughters. From a moral point of view, he did not have the luxury of delaying change until he had achieved more insight, higher self-esteem, or better emotional resolution of his divorce. During the first therapy session, I introduced my concerns about the bind his children must be feeling. During the second and third sessions, after listening empathetically and establishing a genuine therapeutic bond with Joe—he knew I cared about him and wanted to help him—I challenged Joe to take prompt action to undo the damage his stance was doing to his children and to take full responsibility for blackmailing them emotionally.

Earlier in my career, I would have been afraid to challenge someone like Joe in moral terms. What if he collapsed in guilt and shame, or became enraged and dropped out of therapy? What if he agreed in order to placate me but did not follow through with real change? Somewhat to my surprise, I have not encountered these reactions. The keys, in my view, are caring and timing. When I encourage or challenge a client in the moral realm, I do it with full compassion for the powerful personal binds that can lead us all to compromise our moral beliefs, along with a sense of appropriate timing about when to listen and support, when to raise questions, and when to challenge. In his personal insecurity and terror about losing his children, Joe was losing his moral compass, which for years had pointed him toward commitment to his daughters even in the absence of loyalty bonds with their mother.

My challenge to Joe addressed the moral sensibilities he already had.[4] He loved his daughters and would not purposefully harm them. When I showed him the harm he was doing—and invited his daughters into a therapy session to say it for themselves—Joe accepted responsibility without exaggerated self-reproach and immediately set about mending the damage by reassuring his daughters that he would love them always and that they could relate to their stepfather however they wanted. Joe recovered his moral compass and lifted from his daughters a burden they could not have continued to carry and remained emotionally healthy. And the moral fabric of a family had been resewn with a stronger thread of commitment.

Not all cases are as straightforward as Joe's, partly because Joe was a good father who was temporarily impaired by jealousy. I was appealing to a value he held close to his heart: to be there for his children no matter what.

The most frequent expression of moral issues in therapy involves not a challenge by the therapist, as in the cases above, but rather acknowledgment and affirmation of the client's moral language and moral sensibilities. When a female client I was seeing in family therapy reported, during the check-in at the beginning of the session, that she had just come from visiting her dying mother in the nursing home, she added: "I know she was not a very good mother in many ways, but now that she is dying I feel an obligation to be there for her." I replied, simply, "Of course you do." This is a simple affirmation of her moral sensibilities.

An elderly woman who was learning to be more assertive with her husband of fifty years came to a session worried about whether she was being "fair" to him by being more assertive. (He had declined to participate in the therapy.) Ten years ago, I would have suggested to her that fairness was not the issue; rather, the issue would have been something like her personal sense of power, or her use of appropriate assertiveness skills, or whether her efforts were paying off in terms of relational change and her own happiness. Now my first response to her moral question was, "That's an important question. What kinds of things are you doing that you think might be unfair to your husband?" After some discussion, she came to her own conclusion that she was feeling skittish about her new assertiveness but that it was not unfair to her husband to be speaking up for herself for the first time. She was not taking advantage of her lifelong companion; indeed, he seemed happier overall these days, although he disapproved of her being in therapy.

One might think that supporting clients' spontaneous moral expressions is a completely obvious thing to do. Unfortunately, it is not. After a professional presentation during which I told the story of trying to affirm the woman who felt a sense of commitment to her dying mother, a professional in the audience told me about a similar situation, when she herself had been in therapy with a highly regarded therapist during the time her own mother was dying. When she told her therapist of her sense of obligation to help her mother during her last months, the therapist challenged her with the question, "What is she to you now?" This is a classic illustration of egocentric therapeutic morality at work: every expression of obligation is unhealthy until proven otherwise, and every relationship should be measured by its current rewards and costs.

Many therapists would agree that commitment to children and commitment to frail parents are moral issues in therapy, but what about marital commitment? (By marriage I mean sexually bonded relationships in which two individuals have decided to be permanent life partners.) The reining clinical assumption about couples considering divorce might be expressed as follows: Is each partner getting back enough for what he or she is putting into it? Certainly this kind of bottom-line thinking is not only valid but has particular relevance for women, who historically have been discouraged from asserting their self-interest in marriage. Nevertheless, missing from most clinical discussions of divorce is any consideration of moral issues about faithfulness to marriage vows and responsibility to children. The great fear, of course, is that such talk in therapy could serve to entrap people in toxic and even dangerous marriages.

In her book *Uncoupling*, the sociologist Diane Vaughan describes how clients sometimes use therapists as "transition figures" to make an exit from a marriage, particularly when they are in individual therapy.[5] Therapists treating individuals who are in distressed marriages are in a powerful position to encourage or discourage marital commitment. The assumptions embedded in the very language of therapy can move people away from their marital commitment. Every time therapists ask questions on the order of "What are you getting out of this marriage?" and "Why are you staying?" they implicitly encourage divorce by focusing on a self-interested cost-benefit analysis of what the client is deriving from the relationship.

The experience of a friend illustrates therapists' bias against responsible commitments. She went to a well-regarded psychotherapist after her husband of twenty-one years, with whom she had had three children, announced he was having an affair and wanted a separation. The husband then proceeded to fall apart emotionally and had to be hospitalized shortly thereafter. Just three weeks into this marital crisis, my friend's therapist told her that her desire to work to salvage the marriage reflected an "inability to mourn" and a "reluctance to get on with her life." Fortunately, she fired the therapist and got into marital therapy with her husband; they worked it out together.

I want to be clear here: self-interest is a valid and even necessary component of a marital commitment decision. My concern is that self-interest is often the only language accepted in therapy when an individual is making the fateful decision about ending a marriage. Many therapists will dismiss as a cop-out a client's statement that he or she is staying married "for the children's sake," or because "I made a commitment for better or worse." These reasons for staying in a marriage are seen as excuses to avoid making a hard decision based on one's own needs. I certainly thought that way during the 1970s and early 1980s, when I would urge clients to focus on their own needs when deciding whether to stay married or get divorced—the kids would be fine if the parents were fine. I am now willing to recognize and honor clients' moral considerations in making the tortuous decisions that thoughts of marital separation almost always entail. The next case illustrates the power of moral commitment in sustaining a troubled marriage.

When Judith and Steve came to me for marital therapy, they were at one of the lowest points in a marriage that had seen few high points. Judith was a part-time hospital nurse, and Steve was a mechanic. After fifteen years of marriage and three children, ages twelve, ten, and six, Judith and Steve were each terribly frustrated with the other. Steve, who was beginning to understand the distortions in his family history and his personality, felt that Judith alternately abandoned him and treated him like her patient. Judith, who was recovering from years of verbal abuse from Steve, had little tolerance for his complaints about her.

Although the therapy was tough and slow-going, often going

one step forward then two steps back, I was amazed at their persistence. They were one of the more troubled couples I had worked with, but they stubbornly refused to move toward divorce. Earlier in my career, I might have precipitated a crisis in the therapy—"either make progress or let's quit"—but I found myself hanging in there with them, encouraged by their occasional periods of progress.

After the third or fourth major relapse during the first year of therapy, I told them that I was running out of ideas about how to help them and asked if they wanted to continue to see me. They both insisted that they did not want a divorce because it was antithetical to their Jewish values and because it would harm their children. We talked about what sustained their commitment, and they explained that their lives centered on the religious rituals, especially the weekly sabbath meals they held no matter what the state of their relationship. They felt that these rituals provided a glue that helped them stay bonded during the rough periods. Judith and Steve had internalized a powerful and important prescription from their Jewish heritage: the integrity of marriage and family life is too important to compromise without a sustained, energetic, and even stubborn effort to maintain it. I chose not to pathologize their refusal to give up on their marriage.

I told Judith and Steve that I respected their persistence and courage and that if they wanted to continue to work on their marriage, I would work with them. This seemed to galvanize their renewed efforts, which produced the longest sustained period of intimacy in their marriage. I did nothing differently in therapy; we just kept working on their ability to identify their needs, negotiate openly and fairly, and keep the children out of their problems. It was like coaching a losing football team that had decided its problem was not the personnel but how hard the team worked.

Judith and Steve emerged from therapy with a marriage that not only was no longer emotionally debilitating but also gave them a good measure of joy and satisfaction. I expect I will see them from time to time in the future to help them over rough spots.

They don't have a great marriage, and they will always have trouble dealing with conflicts that trigger old vulnerabilities. But they regard their relationship as a "good-enough" marriage, one grounded in their commitment to each other and their children and in their mutual determination to make it work even if it is not the marriage they had hoped for in their youth.

I like to present a case like Judith and Steve's to my graduate students and ask whether they are neutral about people staying married or getting divorced. Generally, the students say that they would support whatever direction clients want to take. But what if clients are uncertain about the question of separating or trying to fix their marriage in therapy? Are they neutral then? Most say yes. Then I ask whether they are as neutral on the question of marital commitment as they would be on the question of, say, whether a client switches jobs from the county government to the city government, or from IBM to Control Data. The latter decisions are lifestyle and career advancement decisions that generally do not carry heavy moral weight. The decision to end a marriage—especially if there are dependent children but even if there are not—is a thoroughly moral issue because of the promises made, the life structure in place, and the consequences for others.

As therapists, we are moral consultants, not just psychosocial consultants. We should not try to impose our beliefs on undecided clients, but we can advocate in an open manner when appropriate. Provided there is no abuse or intimidation, in most cases I tell clients who are considering divorce that I will help them look at their situation and make their own decision, but that I will be leaning toward seeing if it is possible to restore the viability of the marriage. I do not conduct a neutral marital assessment, as if I were a garage mechanic checking out an old car and helping an owner decide whether to repair it or junk it. I look for areas of strength, sniffing for the presence of hope in the midst of pessimism, listening for clues for change. If clients ultimately decide on a divorce, I accept their decision and, if they have children, move on to discuss how they can maintain their commitment as coparents to their children. If they decide to try marital therapy to restore their relationship, I tell them that I will be an advocate for their marriage, as well as for each of them individually, and that I will continue to advocate for their marriage until one or both of them calls me off. In these ways I support the value of marital commitment, a moral issue about which I am not neutral, in the context of respect for clients as moral agents of their own lives.[6]

I am not arguing that marital commitment means that marriage is always forever no matter what. Not all couples can work out the commitment that Judith and Steve did. Consider the case of David and Martha. Married for twelve years, they had a ten-year-old son and a seven-year-old daughter. David was a successful lawyer, and Martha stayed at home with the children. Their marriage had been reasonably satisfying for the first six years, although they were not particularly good at talking through their problems. When David became anxious and moody about his work situation, he tended to become critical of Martha, who then would feel responsible for making him feel better. Instead of speaking up for her own needs and concerns, she would then typically retreat into her cocoon. But they were both very involved with their children and, compared with many of the couples they knew, seemed to have a satisfactory life together.

Things began to change when Martha, after years of unchallenging part-time jobs, decided that she wanted to pursue a fine arts degree. David was supportive of Martha's decision and even sought employment in the geographic area where she wanted to study. The real problem emerged when she actually began school, had less time to be with David, and became what he considered more "liberal" in her social, religious, and political views. As she changed, he accused her of neglecting him and adopting "weird" values. She responded defensively, saying that she had the right to be her own person, and withdrew further from him.

As the atmosphere became more tense, David became anxious and depressed and Martha alternated between vigorously asserting her independence and guiltily reassuming her role as caretaker. She could not give him what he wanted—a return to her old self and an absorption in him and his life. She begged him to go to therapy with her, but for over a year he refused.

When they finally did come to see me, David was mired in his conviction that Martha had become a different and irresponsible person. He gave her lectures about the importance of commitment in marriage and chastised her for making so many destabilizing changes. Martha could not decide about continuing or ending the marriage but was willing to commit to a period of marital therapy to see whether the relationship could be improved. She was miserable, but she was also worried about David's mental health and the welfare of the children. Yet she seriously doubted whether she could stay in the marriage and maintain her own emotional health.

David, for his part, clearly wanted to stay married but did not accept the woman his wife had become. Unlike Martha, he did not recognize or acknowledge his own contributions to the marital problems. The closest he would come was to admit that his job took too much of his time and that being a lawyer had not encouraged him to develop much emotional sensitivity. In their struggle, he saw himself as occupying the higher moral ground because he wanted to preserve the marriage. His agenda in marital therapy was to convince Martha—and me—that she needed to change her ways. He was not interested in self-examination or self-change. Meanwhile, Martha was emotionally drowning in the situation.

Although the details vary, this is not an uncommon scenario for divorce: one spouse has changed in important ways that the other spouse finds unacceptable, and the two of them make things worse when they talk about it. What this couple taught me about the morality of marital commitment is that commitment means more than the willingness to stay married. It was clear that Martha was the initiator of a possible breakup. However, she had responded earlier to the growing marital crisis by seeking therapy a year before they saw me. At that time, David had told her that the problem was hers, not his, and he refused to seek help with her. David's lack of commitment to working on the marriage was fateful: by the time he was willing to participate in therapy, the marriage was terminally ill.

After twenty sessions failed to budge the marital relationship from the destructive zone to the good-enough zone, I ultimately supported Martha's decision to end the marriage. Divorce, I have come to believe, is like an amputation: to be prevented and avoided with all vigor and persistence, but to be done cleanly and decisively when all efforts to keep the body intact have been exhausted. Similarly, I believe that it is irresponsible to end a marriage without attempting marital therapy to see if it can be restored to health—just as it is considered irresponsible to let a loved one die without seeking medical help. However, when a couple has made a mighty effort and both are still miserable and demoralized in their marriage, I can actively support their decision to end it; sometimes people hang on too long after the patient is dead and need encouragement to have a funeral, mourn their losses, and start a new life.

Years later, David made his peace with Martha's decision to end the marriage and realized that he had contributed to the problems. He and Martha have been able to remain committed to their children and to coparent responsibly and effectively since the divorce. With these sustained commitments to their children and to each other as coparents, I believe that they and their children are better off than they would have been staying in a deadly marriage in which their emotional lives and their parenting would have continued to deteriorate to levels perhaps beyond mending.[7]

The most common concern I hear about the explicit use of moral discourse in psychotherapy revolves around the question of whose morality should be introduced. Who decides what is right and wrong in any given situation? Is the therapist expected to have cornered the market on which actions are consistent with moral commitment and which undermine it? When is a divorce an escape from one's adult responsibilities and when is it a necessary, though sometimes tragic, act of moral courage? When is placing an elderly parent in a nursing home an act of abandonment and when is it an act of responsibility? Who gets to decide what is right and wrong?

The exploration of moral issues in therapy does not occur mainly inside the head of the therapist playing moral philosopher or moral judge. It occurs in the heart of the therapeutic dialogue, in conversations in which the therapist listens, reflects, acknowledges, questions, probes, and challenges—and in which the client is free to do the same and to develop a more integrated set of moral sensibilities. Morality emerges for all of us from social interaction punctuated by moments of personal reflection. Morality, in the words of the sociologist Alan Wolfe, is "socially constructed": "Morality thus understood is neither a fixed set of rules handed down unchanging by powerful structures nor something that is made up on the spot. It is a negotiated process through which individuals, by reflecting periodically on what they have done in the past, try to ascertain what they ought to do next. . . . Moral obligation [is] a socially constructed practice."[8]

Morality viewed as a social construction differs from the conservative view of morality as "adherence to rules of conduct shaped by tradition and respect for authority."[9] Those established traditions and authorities have been undermined too extensively to serve as unquestioned arbiters of personal morality in the late twentieth century, except insofar as their precepts make sense to modern men and women. To use an obvious example, all the major monotheistic religions once accepted slavery—now considered a moral evil of staggering proportions—as a practice in keeping with God's will and traditional religious texts. Similarly, governments have manipulated citizens' loyalty and sense of duty to country to have them fight wars that later were commonly considered unjust. The hard-won battle for personal freedom of conscience in the Western world is hardly likely to be followed by a return to an older morality based on unreflective rule-following. And psychotherapists would betray their mission if they saw themselves primarily as agents of moral socialization for established traditions.

On the other hand, I do not believe, as some liberals do, that each individual creates his or her own morality out of whole cloth. We are born into families and communities and ethical-religious traditions that shape us and become part of our identity. As Wilson asserts, each person's moral sensibilities are formed in the intimate environment of family life in childhood and later through wider interactions. This is not to say that we do not distill a personal moral perspective as we mature, but that our moral development and our moral sensibilities are inextricably connected with social interaction. Wilson writes that we are coming "face to face with a fatally-flawed assumption of many Enlightenment thinkers, namely, that autonomous individuals can freely choose, or will, their moral life."[10] Morality is a communal as well as a personal affair.

This overemphasis on autonomy and underemphasis on relationships is one reason Lawrence Kohlberg's very influential theory of moral development, which is related to the liberal political philosophy of John Rawls, is not especially useful to psychotherapy, in my view. His theory focuses on abstract moral principles and on categorizing individuals' moral reasoning into developmental stages.[11] For the purposes of psychotherapy, Kohlberg's work does not deal enough with the affective, interactional, and behavioral aspects of morality—with how people learn, feel, and practice their morality. Even in moral reasoning, its focal area, the model has tended to devalue relational thinking, as Carol Gilligan and others have pointed out.[12] Furthermore, it would be dangerous for therapists to view themselves as leading clients to a "higher" stage of moral development, presumably one occupied by the therapist and not by the client.

Conservatives' rigid rule-following and liberals' excessive individualism and reliance on abstract reasoning, then, do not offer reliable guides for moral discourse in psychotherapy. I believe that a better tradition comes from the early-twentieth-century sociologist George Herbert Mead and other "symbolic-interactionists" who emphasized the social construction of reality.[13] Alan Wolfe's work comes out of that tradition. If morality is created through social interaction, then psychotherapy can be viewed as a form of specialized social interaction in which current moral beliefs and sensibilities are explored, affirmed, revised, or rejected and new ones are created. The therapist, who is also a member of a moral community of social discourse, helps clients reflect on the moral dimensions of their lives.[14] The therapist neither dictates moral rules nor claims to know all the answers, but rather is sensitive to the often delicate interplay of personal, familial, and community needs and responsibilities involved in difficult moral choices.

In the realm of moral responsibility, I do not believe that the therapist's task is to help clients think through their decisions by means of the abstract moral principles that ethicists debate, although these principles have a place in the spectrum of moral discourse. Rather, our major emphasis should be on the lived experience of the moral agent in the late twentieth century, on working through the moments of struggle and pain involved in deciding on the right thing to do. Just as therapists do not supply clients with feelings and desires but rather help clients discover and work better with them, the same is true for moral beliefs and sensibilities. The client brings to therapy the moral raw material that we work with collaboratively; people are continually explaining and justifying their own behavior and evaluating the morality of others' behavior. The therapist is a consultant in this ongoing process of moral reflection.

Here are four examples of everyday moral concerns that came up in a week's worth of psychotherapy in my practice:

- A man's justification for not visiting his elderly mother anymore was that she had become so negative that visits upset him for days afterward.
- Because she felt stultified and unable to grow as a person in her marriage, a woman felt justified in seeking a divorce.
- Another woman justified her decision to divorce on the grounds that her husband had betrayed her trust in many ways over the course of many years.
- A teenage boy told his parents that it was unfair to penalize him for the disruptive behavior of his younger siblings.

Like all of us, these individuals have a basic "moral sense" or "moral sensibility," which Wilson defines as "an intuitive or directly felt belief about how one ought to act when one is free to act voluntarily (that is, not under duress). . . . Most of us have a moral sense, but . . . some of us have tried to talk ourselves out of it."[15] It is time for psychotherapists to stop trying to talk people out of their moral sense.

Two large gaps in my discussion so far point to issues I address in later chapters. The first is the role of the community and social institutions in the social construction of morality, and the difficulty in conducting a morally sensitive therapy in a morally opaque or exploitative community context. The second is preparing therapists to be sensitive to the special context and experiences of clients, especially when the therapist and the client do not share the same moral community. These issues have important implications for reenvisioning the role and training of the psychotherapist in contemporary society.

To recap, I am arguing that there is a good fit between the view of morality as a social construction and the view of psychotherapy as a form of social interaction in which moral conversation and moral consultation can occur more explicitly than therapists have allowed in the past.

If therapists are to be useful moral consultants—and I believe we are moral consultants whether we claim to be or not—we will have to uncover and evaluate our moral beliefs and moral sensibilities more self-consciously than we have in the past. For example, each therapist will need to develop a stance on the issue of moral relativism. Are all differences of opinion on moral issues simply differences in personal preference or personal taste? Are all practices approved within a given culture morally acceptable? Are not all moral beliefs expressions of a particular context and therefore unimpeachable from outside that context? The social constructionist view of morality can be taken to imply an extreme relativism, as if whatever emerges from social interaction is inherently worthwhile from an ethical standpoint. I do not believe this is so. While I am aware that my beliefs are shaped by my gender, race, sexual orientation, social class, religion, culture, and time in history, I don't believe that all moral beliefs are created equal. The moral consensus of the world's major religions around the Golden Rule—do unto others as you would have others do unto you—is a far better guide to moral living than the reflexive morality of self-interest in mainstream American society.

Of course, in my role as a modern secular therapist, I cannot back up my nonrelativist beliefs with an appeal to an external authority that my client and I are bound to accept, such as a religious text. (Pastoral counselors, however, can refer to such texts when working with people from their own religious tradition.)[16] Thus, when my client and I differ in our moral sensibilities, I cannot pull moral rank. I am a consultant whose position can be ignored or rejected by my client. The exception is when the client has committed a crime, such as child abuse, which I am required by law to report, thereby acting as an agent of social control—and more than likely precipitating the end of the therapeutic relationship.

By not pulling moral rank, I am not talking about "feel-good" moral consultation, that is, never challenging or angering the client. Sometimes a client will be quite uncomfortable with the therapist's questions or comments about moral matters. Once in a while a client may drop out of therapy because he or she senses a large values gap. However, I also think there are some clients these days who fire therapists they experience as promoting an ethic of self-interest at the expense of loved ones—as with a client of mine whose previous therapist had told her in the first session of individual therapy that her husband would never change and she would have to decide whether to leave him. She was appalled at the therapist's attitude toward her commitment to a chronically ill man to whom she had been married for thirty-five years. This not-unfamiliar story bespeaks how the therapist-client relationship can become the casualty of a values difference when the therapist is consciously trying to be value-free. I believe that the number of such casualties will decline when therapists become more aware of how their values and moral beliefs affect their work, and when they are willing to openly discuss differences with clients.

Psychotherapy is a form of conversation, and moral consultation in psychotherapy can range from the mildest affirmations to the most intense challenges. Following are eight types of responses I have used with clients in dealing with moral issues, listed in increasing order of intensity. I include brief examples drawn from the issue of family commitment. It is important to keep in mind that these moments of moral conversation punctuate otherwise regular clinical interactions. Some of the examples may not be consistent with every therapist's mode of doing therapy; they are not intended to be prescriptive but rather to make more concrete the range of statements related to moral responsibility that I use in therapy.

1. *Validate the language of moral concern when clients use it spontaneously.* A noncustodial father of school-age children was

pondering whether to take a job in a city far away from his children. He wondered whether his move would hurt his ability to be a good father to them. I affirmed that indeed this was a very important concern.

2. *Introduce language to make more explicit the moral horizon of the client's concern.* The father in the above example proceeded to frame the issue in terms of the possible damage to his "relationship" with his children, a category that does not necessarily encompass the possible harm to the children and the importance of his one-way commitment to them. I sensed that his concern was deeper than his language implied, and I said, "Yes, they may feel that you are walking out of their lives by moving away." My response focused the subsequent discussion more clearly around the needs of the children.

3. *Ask questions about clients' perceptions of the consequences of their actions on others, and explore the personal, familial, and cultural sources of these moral sensibilities.* A woman suddenly left her second husband and moved into a small apartment where her teenage children could not live, leaving them with their stepfather. Her daughter in particular was very distressed. After empathetically listening to the woman's story, I asked, "When you were making a decision to leave, how did you think it would affect your children? And how do you think they feel now?" Her answer led to a discussion in which she indicated she had not anticipated the hurt and pain her children would experience and to an exploration of what she could do now to repair the damage.

4. *Articulate the moral dilemma without giving your own position.* In the case of the woman who moved out on her children, I arranged a session with her, her children, and the stepfather. (The therapy had been initiated to address the daughter's distress.) After the daughter spoke openly about how rejected she felt when her mother moved to a place where

her children could not live even part-time, the mother explained that she had felt a need to start a new life and moving to a friend's small apartment seemed to be the most logical way to get out quickly. I then framed the dilemma as follows (speaking to the mother): "So, on the one hand, you've got your strong personal need to leave your marriage right away, and on the other hand, you've got your children's need to be with you as their mother and to know that you want them." I let the family take the ball from there.

5. *Bring research findings and clinical insight to bear on the consequences of certain actions, particularly for vulnerable individuals.* Although such information can be presented in any therapy situation, here I am referring to the use of data and theory to influence clients to take a course of action that the therapist considers morally better as well as psychosocially healthier. For example, in speaking to Bruce about whether to leave his children after his marital separation, I described the research data on the importance of regular, predictable contact between fathers and children after divorce. I was summarizing data not as an objective scientist but as a moral exhorter.

6. *Describe how you generally see the issue and how you tend to weigh the moral options, emphasizing that every situation is unique and that the client will, of course, make his or her own decision.* A man was contemplating leaving his wife because the marriage had been empty for him for many years. He had never told her how unhappy he was. He was trying to decide whether to start marital therapy or to end the marriage right away. After exploring his feelings and his thinking, I said something like, "I'll tell you the position I have come to over the years on the question of pulling the plug on the marriage right away versus trying marital therapy. Now bear in mind that I am a marital therapist, so I am not objective here. But my view is that a long-term marriage is too important a thing to give up on without a serious effort to

salvage it in marital therapy. I'm sure there are exceptions, and I can't tell you that you should try therapy or that it will work. But I hate to see a couple break up without at least some consideration of getting help together." He decided to bring in his wife, and in this case the therapy was successful.

7. *Say directly how concerned you are about the moral consequences of the client's actions.* This is what I did with Bruce when he was contemplating a quick move out of town and out of his children's lives. Because time was short, a decision was imminent, and I had a good relationship with him, I used an intense form of moral response.

8. *Clearly state when you cannot support a client's decision or behavior, explaining your decision on moral grounds and, if necessary, withdrawing from the case.* A couple had started marital therapy, and the wife told me privately that she had an ongoing, intense romantic relationship with another man, one that had been sexual but for the time being (perhaps only for a short time) was not sexual. She did not want her husband to know about it but believed she could give marital therapy a good effort. I told her that I could not accept her decision to participate in marital therapy without telling her husband about the other relationship, because it would be unfair to him to be in the dark when she and I knew about her divided commitment. Having made the moral point, I also told her that I was confident that the therapy would not be successful in any event if she had an outside lover. The latter remark spoke to the pragmatic consideration I was trained to address—the former spoke to the moral consideration I had to learn to speak up about. After I made a stand about not doing the couples therapy, she decided to tell her husband about the relationship and to end it while therapy continued.

Our therapy caseloads are like Shakespearean dramas suffused with moral passion and moral dilemmas. We have been trained to see Romeo and Juliet only as starstruck, tragic lovers, a perspective from which we fail to notice that the moral fabric of parental commitment was torn when their families rejected them for loving each other. We focus on the murder of Hamlet's father and Hamlet's own existential crisis, rather than on Hamlet's mother's abandonment of her grieving son. Commitment to loved ones and betrayal of that commitment are central moral themes in the human drama played out in psychotherapy every day. For Bruce, a searing divorce was the moral crucible in which he forged a new identity as a committed, loving father who could give without counting the returns and remain faithful without weighing the alternatives. From the moment Bruce told me he might abandon his children, I knew that the therapy was about more than psychological and family issues; it was about Bruce's moral integrity and about the moral fabric of a family. That revelation changed both of us.

CHAPTER 3

Justice

MOST OF THE MEN IN MY MEN'S GROUPS HAVE HAD disastrous experiences with marriage and other close relationships with women. These men are often unassertive with their ex-wives and ex-lovers and have been left feeling taken advantage of and pushed around. Rather than diving directly into the threatening waters of another relationship with a woman, they generally learn how to take support from other men on the shore, and how to do friendships better.

Issues of justice or fairness come up in these groups, just as they do elsewhere in psychotherapy. Elliott's ex-wife frequently insulted him in front of the children when he went to pick them up, calling him insensitive and irresponsible. She also spent money impulsively and expected him to bail her out when she could not pay the mortgage or fix the car (he always came up with the money). Elliott would recount these stories with more resignation than anger, whereupon the group would express outrage about how unfairly he was being treated and consternation about his not standing up for himself.

One way of dealing with justice in therapy involves helping clients perceive how they are being exploited and empowering them to assert their rights and needs. Sometimes the injustice is personal and localized, as in Elliott's case. Clients who are members of groups that are discriminated against or oppressed in the larger society—such as women, homosexuals, and people of color—can be helped by a therapist to stop blaming themselves for the effects in their lives of unfair social conditions. The shame of being laid off from work and forced onto welfare can be ameliorated by the realization that the economic world is often organized to promote the welfare of the few at the expense of the many. In an unjust world, therapists can help people view their personal pain through a wider lens than that of personal failing or family dysfunction.[1]

The work of the psychiatrist and family therapist Ivan Boszormenyi-Nagy is instructive here. For more than three decades, Boszormenyi-Nagy has been developing a theory and clinical model based on justice in family relations as a core factor in mental health and illness. Boszormenyi-Nagy believes that the experience of injustice—when parents take too much and give too little to their children—has a corrosive influence on human development. Adults who grew up in such families often have a sense of "destructive entitlement": they use and abuse other people in a misguided attempt to redress the inequities of childhood. They view the world as divided into the exploited and the exploiters, and they know whom they prefer. They are not able to give to the next generation because the balance of justice—of giving and receiving—has been so distorted in their lives. Notwithstanding romantic myths of how conscience develops under the searing heat of injustice and oppression, the experience of injustice corrodes rather than ennobles most human lives.[2]

A central task of psychotherapy, then, is to help clients come to grips with their own experiences of injustice. Sometimes this involves bringing to the surface feelings about a father who abandoned his children or a mother who was physically abusive. The experience of sexual abuse in the home is a particularly profound instance of injustice, one that requires considerable exploration and healing. Often the early stages of therapy with such exploited clients focus on helping them externalize the anger and outrage that they have internalized in the form of self-loathing. They learn that as a child they were in no way responsible for their unjust victimization. At a later stage of therapy, they may come to understand their abusive parent's own history of being exploited and may develop a way to accept the good part of that parent while rejecting the bad. This two-step process—of accepting as real one's experience of injustice and later crediting what can be credited to the parent—is at the heart of Boszormenyi-Nagy's model of treating adults who have been victimized in their families.

Although this way of dealing with justice—helping people perceive and respond to unjust treatment in their personal world—is often a challenging task in therapy, it has been very familiar ground to therapists for decades. There are clinical theories and techniques to guide us, as well as many workshops on helping clients recover from a variety of unjust experiences. Examining the destructive role of larger systems of injustice and oppression is a newer frontier in psychotherapy, practiced mostly by feminist therapists and therapists of color (more on this issue in chapter 5). However, both the private focus and the public focus deal with the client as a victim of injustice, not as a potential agent of injustice. That is, neither deals explicitly with the fairness or unfairness of the client's own behavior.[3] This much less familiar ground is fraught with dangers for the therapeutic relationship. In the following case, I took my first big risk in challenging a client for contemplating an unjust action.

Paul had been complaining in a men's therapy group about how difficult it was to manage his three young children on weekends in his small apartment. Never a good disciplinarian, Paul now had to cope with his children away from their friends, toys, and private spaces. He began to dread their visits. Although the group and I offered to help him with child-care ideas, he expressed doubts that his children could change, given how their mother spoiled them at home.

Once in a while, Paul had a good weekend with his children when he had just two of the three. I remember well the day when Paul, looking self-satisfied, told the group that he had figured out a way to improve his weekends with his children. He would take only two of them at a time, in rotation. When asked if his ex-wife would go along with this, he replied that he thought he could talk her into it. She would agree if he made a case for the children's need for quality time with him. She was a sucker, it seemed, for arguments in terms of the children's needs and would not give much immediate thought to the consequences for her own child-care commitments.

The group congratulated Paul on this creative way of managing his stress while improving his time with his children. There was no sympathy for his ex-wife, Susan, given how badly she had treated him at the time of separation. Paul was going to talk with her that night about his plan.

I set off a bomb in this cozy group process when I said I was concerned about how this arrangement would affect Susan. Paul admitted that she would not have any weekends free from child care but quickly added that she had plenty of relatives who could help out—and besides, she had already found time for a personal vacation with a friend. I said, "I have to question whether this is fair to her. If she agrees, she will never be free of responsibility, never get a break from children. I'm concerned that she may let herself get talked into an arrangement that will be harmful for her over the long run—and harmful to the children if she goes under."

There was a rush of anger from the group. I had crossed over a boundary in therapeutic discourse by advocating for fairness to an enemy. Group members muttered statements such as, "Who cares what happens to her?" and, "That's her problem," and, "She'd do the same to him." One especially articulate group member challenged me by saying, "I thought you were here to help *us*, the people in this room. She's not your client; we are." Paul, looking pained but interested, asked me to say more.

I told the group that I realized they did not expect this from me as a therapist because generally I did indeed advocate for them, but that I had to be concerned about the other people in their lives. I thought what Paul was contemplating would be harmful to Susan and would probably hurt the children eventually as well. Even if she agreed, she probably had little sense of the long-term burden she was undertaking in never having a weekend free for herself. It wasn't my place to tell Paul what to do, but I said I couldn't be silent when I thought he was contemplating doing something that would harm Susan, even though she was not my client.

This encounter was a turning point for the group, and for me in my work as a therapist. I had never gone so far out on a limb to advocate for fair treatment for someone hated by my client. I was defining myself to Paul and the other group members as a morally concerned therapist, even if doing so meant not supporting Paul's short-term interests. Once I took this stand, however, Paul began to move away from his interest in manipulating his ex-wife. Seemingly without regret or resentment, he decided to maintain the current visitation arrangement and to work harder on his parenting skills. The group too seemed to come to peace with my stance, and it became easier to bring up justice concerns in the sessions.

I am aware that I could probably have accomplished the same goal—preventing Paul from conning his ex-wife into accepting an unjust child-care arrangement—by appealing to his self-interest. For example, I could have pointed out that she might see through his manipulation, or that the arrangement would be likely to fall through when she got overwhelmed and there would then be a lot of conflict about restoring the status quo. In other words, I could have argued from the principle of utility—it wouldn't work as a plan to promote Paul's interests. This is valid reasoning, but using only the discourse of utilitarian self-interest would have implied that I believed the means were morally sound but not practical or effective. What if Paul had said he was considering stealing from her savings account? Should I have responded only by pointing out the likelihood that he would be caught and go to jail? What if Paul thought he had a safe plan to accomplish the deed? At some point wouldn't I have to say, in effect, "I can't support you on this because I think it is wrong to take your ex-wife's money"?

It is easier, of course, for therapists to take moral stands when the law is involved. If a client is contemplating a crime, then the moral lighthouse casts clear illumination. The clinical reality is that clients rarely tell us they are contemplating breaking laws, but they do tell us from time to time about behavior or plans that we believe involve unjust treatment of people in their lives. The central question for therapists is, when is it appropriate to introduce the discourse of justice and fairness in talking about client behavior that is morally, though not legally, suspect?

The response I gave to Paul and the group—a direct statement of concern about the harm his plan would cause his ex-wife—was a number 7 on the 8-step scale of intensity of moral responses I described in chapter 2. It was a quick move to the heart of the ethical concern. Paul was not seeing the issue as a moral one, was being roundly praised by the group for his plan, and was about to implement it that evening. Furthermore, given the time allotments in the group, we had only about twenty minutes to deal with Paul's concerns. For these reasons, I chose to start with a fairly intense form of moral statement.

I believe that putting my concern in the less intense form of a question, such as "What do you think about your needs in this situation versus Susan's?" (moral response number 3), would have been less helpful, for two reasons. First, I could already anticipate Paul's and the group's response: "[Expletive] Susan!" Then, instead of having raised my concern proactively as something I wanted to say, I would be in the position of seeming to reprimand Paul and the group for their hostile attitude. Second, I felt that it would be disingenuous to ask a question that so obviously expressed my own moral position instead of just saying it directly. Questions work better when they do not transparently reflect the therapist's own position. For example, if Paul had said that he wouldn't buy the arrangement if he were in Susan's place, that response would have given me the opening to probe his implicit moral stance: "Why would this be a questionable deal from Susan's point of view?"

The anger I received from the group—not so much from Paul himself, interestingly—is very common when fairness toward an ex-spouse is discussed. Because divorced people who feel ripped off financially and emotionally by their ex-spouse do not like to hear about their ex's rights and needs, my intense moral statement to Paul was risky to the therapeutic relationship, justified though it was, I believe, by the circumstances. More often, I find opportunities to inject the quality of justice into the discussion by using the two mildest forms of moral response (numbers 1 and 2). For example, many clients say that they are trying to make the divorce settlement fair to both parties. I respond, "I can see that fairness is an important standard to you." This simple statement honors and supports a core moral quality in the client, one that he or she may need to access more and more in the coming months.

If the client talks about making reasonable concessions but does not use explicitly ethical language, I might add a comment such as "You seem to be trying to take care of yourself in this process but without taking advantage of your ex." Most clients will respond by more clearly articulating their moral sensibilities about how they want to treat their ex and how they want to be treated in return. Struggling to be fair to someone who has hurt and rejected you, particularly in the context of the adversarial legal system, is one of those bracketed times of moral intensity when a therapist can be a facilitator of genuine moral growth. Or, as so often happens, the therapist can be just one more advocate in an adversarial process whose underlying ethic is often one of legalized warfare.

I want to make it clear that a therapist must help the client advocate for fair treatment for himself or herself. The Golden Rule involves self-protection as well as fair treatment of the other. Nothing in what I am saying should be construed as endorsement of an ex-spouse sacrificing self-interest by making concessions that are not reciprocated. Some clients come prepared to give away the store in order to avoid a struggle; they need help in asserting their rights. Other clients are reeling from outrageously unfair actions by the ex-spouse; they need help in protecting themselves and regaining some initiative.

But self-interest is not a difficult issue for most therapists (and attorneys) to understand. What is difficult, given the orientation of traditional forms of psychotherapy, is affirming or promoting the moral stature of a client who is dealing with strong negative feelings and an urgent need for self-protection. Even if the spouse is being viciously unfair in the divorce process, we have a responsibility to help our clients avoid compromising themselves ethically—for example, by resorting to the same kinds of lies and child manipulation that may characterize the ex's actions. Ethical self-empowerment is what we should promote; anything else undermines the client's moral integrity—and, I think, the therapist's.

Feminism, I have come to believe, is essentially about justice. Women have been treated historically and systematically as second-class human beings, particularly in the public sphere. Beginning in the 1970s, feminist therapists started criticizing the gender-neutral and value-neutral claims of psychotherapy, pointing out the ways in which therapists were unwittingly perpetuating both gender stereotypes and unfair treatment of women. Feminist family therapists in particular showed how therapists often assumed that wives and mothers were mainly responsible for the housework and child-rearing and the emotional maintenance of the marriage. Consistent with the entitlements that men have in the larger society, men in families were often catered to in therapy. It was easier to hold mothers more responsible for family problems—because the internal life of the family was deemed their sphere.[4]

Feminist therapists not only championed the idea of justice in therapy but were also among the first to advocate that therapists be clear and explicit about their own values in therapy. However, some therapists have watered down feminism by using only the language of sex-role training, that is, concerning themselves only with how men and women are socialized differently and communicate differently. The answer they come to is that we just need to understand one another better. The problem with this approach is that it skirts issues of justice and power in marriage and in other systems. Understanding is not sufficient when people are being treated unfairly.

Using the language of justice in therapy can serve double duty by encouraging changes in both women and men, as the next case illustrates. Fran and Steve had a healthy six-year-old boy and a developmentally delayed four-year-old daughter. They came to me for medical family therapy after learning that their daughter would probably never be able to communicate verbally or live independently. They were devastated, and Fran was suffering profound grief and exhaustion. She worked full-time in a retail management position, and Steve ran his own business. Fran handled virtually all of the myriad relationships with health professionals, school professionals, and insurance companies. This work took many hours a week and required constant vigilance and unswerving advocacy for their daughter's rights and needs in three complex bureaucracies, along with the cultivation of good personal relationships with physicians, nurses, teachers, school psychologists, and insurance company gatekeepers. It was like running a separate family business.

Although Steve worked more hours in his business than Fran did in her paid job and was active in the home as a parent, he left the logistics of managing their daughter's medical and educational needs to his wife. When occasionally she pushed him to help more—say, in dealing with an insurance company directly—he would increase his activity for a time, but often she had to help him because she knew much more about the case. Ultimately, it seemed easier for her just to handle things herself than to nag her husband and then supervise his efforts. She was paying a big price in her emotional well-being, however, and her commitment to the marriage was becoming tenuous.

Fran felt trapped because she could not imagine coping as a single parent, and because she thought Steve was a terrific father. Except for the strain of caring for their daughter's problems, their marital relationship was satisfactory. He worked too many evenings when she wanted companionship, and he thought she was on his case too much about it, but these were garden-variety marital gripes, not threats to the marriage. The sword of Damocles hanging over them was the burden of dealing with outside institutions in caring for their daughter's needs.

The first key element in the therapy was helping Fran take a stand about wanting Steve to share the burdens; she was drowning and she deserved a partner. She had to stop excusing him because he worked extra hours in his business, and she had to stop putting herself down for not being superwoman. With my support, she began to speak up for her legitimate need for his active involvement. She started seeing the excessive burden she carried and the marital strain as a matter of justice, not just an issue of whether he cared for her enough to help out when she could no longer cope.

The second key element in the therapy was helping Steve see that it was not fair for his wife to carry all the responsibility for coordinating their daughter's care. This message resonated with Steve, who saw himself as a fair-minded and ethical person who worked hard and did not take advantage of others. When Fran told him in therapy that she needed him to participate more, and that she was ready to give up some control, he responded readily by saying it was time for him to do more—because he could see what was happening to her and because it was the right thing to do.

Instead of describing his added role as "helping" Fran through a rough spot—they had tried this approach on their own, and it didn't last—I framed the matter in terms of an equal balance of responsibility for their home and work lives and a fair sharing of the burdens. Once they agreed in principle to make a shift, I suggested that they start with Steve taking over full responsibility for dealing with a major external burden. Fran proposed that she continue to handle the school issues, since she had a good relationship with the professionals involved. (Their contacts with physicians were now less frequent because their daughter was medically stable.) They agreed that Steve would take on full responsibility for contacts with insurance companies and would consult with her and keep her informed as needed. Steve performed this task with the same workmanlike approach he brought to his business. Their relationship improved markedly, and Fran's sense of being overwhelmed diminished.

My handling of the mechanics of this case was not that different from the approach many therapists would have taken. What was different was my emphasis on the fairness of their family roles. Neither of them came into therapy requesting changes in these roles; they came in because Fran was having a hard time after the bad medical news about their child. Neither of them saw a realistic alternative to their current arrangements. If I had presented Steve's concern for Fran's emotional well-being as the main reason for change—a valid reason to be sure, and one we talked about—I would have failed to deal with the unfairness of their situation. Once Fran felt better, Steve would have felt justified in withdrawing again, the need for his extra care having vanished.

Similarly, if I had focused only on how their relationship might benefit from more sharing—another valid issue we talked about—then there might not have been much staying power in their changes. Indeed, they were in the habit of taking a vacation alone each year, during which they reconnected as a couple; after returning home, Fran would feel better able to cope alone with her excessive burdens and renewed in her desire not to hurt the marriage by pestering Steve to do more. A vacation is a faster route to marital connection than calling insurance companies.

In other words, the appeals to care and intimacy, although important adjuncts to what I worked on, would not have been enough. I believe that these two issues lacked the moral under-girding required to bring about permanent, stable change: it was unfair for Fran to be excessively burdened when Steve had time and energy to spare. They were trapped by traditional gender training into an unjust arrangement that was undermining Fran's personal well-being and their relationship. This injustice mani-fested itself clearly at times, as when Fran suggested that she quit her job to care for their children and Steve insisted that the family needed her salary. They both worked hard, but he carried only a job and a half (being self-employed) while she carried two jobs—and one of them frequently a gut-wrenching experience because it made her face their daughter's profound limitations.

Restoring justice to Fran and Steve's relationship brought about a more sustainable closeness and partnership than they had had since their daughter's birth. Fran no longer lived with self-recrimination and buried resentment toward Steve. And Steve felt renewed pride in actively dealing with the outside world on behalf of his daughter and his family. An additional benefit was that they were more effec-tive as a team in dealing with outside groups. Steve turned out to be very effective in dealing with insurance officials who were unaccus-tomed to working with fathers. And Fran had the time and energy to develop more positive relationships with the school professionals who were working every day with their daughter. Equitable mar-riages make for the best teamwork inside and outside the home.

Appealing to fairness is an untapped resource for therapists in pro-moting gender equality in couples and families. The aim of restoring fairness can give women a firmer foundation for their requests for change than simple appeals to "help her out" when she can't cope. Some women focus too much on criticizing their husbands for selfishness, naturally eliciting defensive responses. Others inconsistently make demands only when they are upset about something. Many times women appeal to an ethic of care in asking men to contribute more to family work when they would be more effective appealing to an ethic of fairness. Carol Gilligan's work supports the observation that men respond more readily to issues of justice and fairness, which are rooted in same-gender play and work relationships from childhood onward, than to issues of caring, which are less prominent in their gender socialization.[5]

I do not want to fall into the trap of holding women responsible for coming up with the "correct" way to talk to men if change is to occur in their marriages, as though everything would then fall into place. Achieving more justice and equality in marriage is not a simple proposition, no matter what the grounds on which the case is made. I am simply suggesting that therapists can work more effectively with couples if they consciously promote the virtue of fairness and help couples articulate their concerns in these terms.

Justice, of course, cuts both ways in cross-gender relationships; men are not the only ones who treat their partners unfairly. When a husband takes over an area of responsibility, his wife sometimes sabotages him by reclaiming it at his first misstep. This is not only a dysfunctional relationship pattern and a form of self-sabotage for the wife, but it is unfair to the husband. He deserves the right to learn by his mistakes. It is not uncommon for women to want to share the work at home but not the power and control, given their traditional socialization to regard the home as their personal domain. The results merely turn the tables of injustice.

When a therapist supports a woman in asserting her right to fair treatment in a relationship with a man, he or she should also be on the lookout for how the female client treats her male partner unfairly as well. Her unfair behavior may occur in other domains of their life, such as withholding sex to manipulate him, or criticizing him to their children or relatives. The therapist needs to advocate for a just relationship for both, not ally with the woman to morally reform the man.

As rich as I believe feminist theory is for guiding therapy, this issue of women's unjust behavior points out one of its limitations. Because feminism arose as an emancipatory movement to free women from oppression by men and patriarchal structures, feminist theories inevitably have difficulty seeing and dealing with unjust and exploitative behavior by women toward others. This is not to say that feminist therapists as individual practitioners ignore women's acts of injustice, but that the lenses of their guiding feminist theories focus much more clearly on the injustices done to women than on the injustices done by women. In the following case, I challenged a woman about her destructive and unfair behavior toward her separated husband and her children.

Marcia and Glen had been married for seventeen years and had a twelve-year-old son and a seventeen-year-old daughter. Both were successful in business. They came to me on the verge of separation after several years of unresolved conflict and tension. She felt he put her down much of the time, and he felt she was explosive and unpredictable. Glen presented a calm, rational front but came across as highly patronizing and dismissive to her in the initial sessions. Marcia presented a very emotional front and wavered back and forth between wanting him to stay and wishing he would leave. The tension and distrust were so high that it was hard for me to work with them.

Early in the therapy, after pointing out Glen's dismissive behavior (he would laugh when she talked and then characterize her as "disturbed") and encouraging Marcia not to sit still for it, I finally took him on directly. I told him that his behavior was so demeaning to Marcia, who was so accustomed to it that she did not react to it, that I could not let him treat her that way in the sessions. It was a galvanizing moment in the therapy, for Glen heard me and modified his behavior considerably, and Marcia understood better what was happening to her. Glen, it turns out, had an image of himself as a decent and fair man—an image inconsistent with his disrespectful behavior toward his wife. But he asked Marcia to stop verbally abusing him outside of therapy.

Marcia admitted that she had an explosive temper and frequently called Glen vicious names and attacked his character. However, she thought her attacks did not hurt him very much—he never showed any pain—and besides, she was an emotional Italian who could not be expected to curb her feelings all the time. Marcia's verbal abuse was more difficult for me to deal with than Glen's, in part because she didn't believe that a "weak" woman like herself could inflict damage on a "powerful" man. She did work on managing her anger for the sake of the relationship, but never with the kind of moral conviction that Glen used—at times anyway—to fuel his efforts to change his behavior.

After several more sessions, Glen moved out. Marcia was devastated and wanted to salvage the marriage. Glen said he was willing to continue for a while in therapy but doubted that the marriage was salvageable. Eventually, he reconfirmed his decision to divorce and initiated proceedings. Marcia felt completely victimized by him for his failure of commitment and wanted to stop therapy. Glen convinced her to continue with the sessions to work out coparenting issues, since he was concerned about the children getting caught in the middle. From the time of the separation, they each had the children half-time.

When I met with the children alone, they told me they liked the arrangement of seeing both parents equally. However, they complained that their mother continually spoke badly of their father; their father did not say bad things about their mother. When I helped the children challenge their mother about this behavior in a family session, she at first dismissed their concerns and then agreed to work on it. I pointed out how unfair it was to the children to be put in the middle, and Marcia concurred. I explained research findings to support this position.

A month later, however, Marcia learned that Glen was dating another woman. A furious Marcia told the children that their father was an adulterer. She threatened Glen with legal action to keep the children away from him. Glen was shocked and dismayed at her reaction, but he promised not to involve the children with the new woman, at least not until the divorce was final and he had a more established relationship with her.

Glen's offer did not mollify Marcia. All of her grief and anger about the failed marriage and about how Glen had treated her over the years came pouring out around the issue of his new relationship. I continued to empathize with her pain but urged her to keep the children out of the conflict. She reluctantly agreed. Then one afternoon, after a session, she called me to say that she couldn't keep her promise to not speak ill of her husband to the children. She had seen her individual therapist that day (she had sought individual therapy when Glen moved out) and asked him how she should handle her powerful anger toward Glen when she talked with her children. She reported that her therapist had said, "Whatever you do, you have to be true to yourself. You cannot lie to them about your feelings."

I was horrified at her therapist's response, and I had to think quickly because she said she was going to have a discussion with her children the next day and planned to tell them that their father was morally unfit and a bad influence on them. More particularly, she intended to tell her son that she didn't want him to grow up to be irresponsible and immoral like his father. The son, I should add, had had considerable behavioral problems throughout the separation and had pleaded with his mother during a session to keep him out of the middle. I told Marcia I could understand the terrible pain, hurt, and betrayal she felt. Then I said, "Marcia, this is a very serious situation, and I am going to say some hard things right now. I may come across as authoritarian, and if I do, I apologize in advance. But I am very concerned that you are about to do something that will be extremely harmful to your children. Saying these things to them about their father will put them at considerable risk. You may feel temporarily better by telling them how you are feeling, but they will carry the burden for a long time."

Marcia softened somewhat but repeated that she could not "lie" to her children; she could not "paint a positive picture of him." She was tired of protecting him. I responded: "I don't want you to lie to your children either, but I think there is a difference between saying something you don't believe—like 'I think your father is a great guy,' which would be a lie—and saying everything you think about him. You owe it to your children not to lie to them about their father [she agreed wholeheartedly], but you do not owe your children full disclosure of all your negative opinions about him. As for not painting a positive picture of him, you don't have to paint a picture of him at all. Just don't talk about him with the children. Then you don't have to lie, but you won't get them in the middle."

These words got through to Marcia, who calmed down and agreed not to "vent" with her children. Using the most intense moral responses at my disposal, I was appealing to her caring and fair side, which had become overwhelmed by her pain and grief. She had treated the children too much like confidants during the marriage and was understandably predisposed to say too much to them now. It was not an easy adjustment for Marcia, and she knew I understood that. In a couple of months, we ended our sessions as the divorce progressed and the coparental tensions diminished.

The other therapist's words are particularly frightening when I think back on this case. In her emotional hurt, despite her obvious love for her children, Marcia was contemplating a great act of injustice: sabotaging their relationship with their father. This act would have been as wrong as any form of child abuse. But her therapist, at least according to Marcia's report, responded to her dilemma, like Polonius advising Hamlet, in terms of Marcia's need for authenticity: to thine own self be true. As if the greatest evil to avoid in this situation was to not be "real." This is moral discourse stripped of its interpersonal connections, reduced to a morality of expressive individualism. It is no different from a financial adviser urging a corporate client, faced with an ethical dilemma about polluting the environment, to consider only the immediate needs of the stockholders.

The case of Marcia and her family raises again the important issue of timing in dealing with moral issues in therapy, especially the timing of the therapist's more intense moral responses. Listening, reflecting, and affirming must precede any ethical challenge in psychotherapy; clients must know that we have heard them and care about them. Furthermore, the client must have responded positively to some other clinical challenge in the nonmoral domain, such as a challenge to examine distorted beliefs or unacknowledged feelings, or to try out a new, probably uncomfortable behavior. In other words, moral challenge (response numbers 7–8) requires a reasonably well-functioning therapeutic relationship in which the therapist's nurturing and challenging have both proven acceptable to the client.

The same principle applies to the timing of a moral challenge during an individual therapy session: the client must have the sense of being heard and understood and sympathized with, and be open to input, before the therapist's moral challenge is likely to be helpful. On the other hand, I believe that introducing moral discourse at less intense levels as a regular part of a therapist's repertoire greatly facilitates the usefulness and acceptability of more intense moral responses when they are necessary. I had frequently discussed fairness issues with Marcia and Glen, and my convictions were no surprise to her. In fact, I believe she called me precisely to hear my appeal to her conscience as against her desire for vengeance.

Besides timing, the other crucial issue is what to do when the client doesn't buy what you are saying. The central distinction between a moralistic therapy and a morally sensitive therapy, between moral pedagogy and moral consultation, is revealed by the therapist's response when the client disagrees with the therapist's moral position, perhaps even decides to act counter to the therapist's suggestion. Except when there is grave and present danger to someone's well-being, the therapist as moral consultant will explore the areas of diverging opinions and then back off. Clients usually think about the issues raised on their own and not infrequently raise them again in future sessions. Therapists do not want to become someone clients are accountable to for their ethical decisions—a sure prescription for avoiding honest disclosure about their behavior. If, after my urgent challenge, Marcia had told her children what she had been planning to tell them, I would not have criticized her or questioned her ethics but would have worked with her and the children to try to minimize the damage and to help Marcia do better by them the next time she was furious at her ex-husband. The central safeguard for keeping moral consultation from becoming prescriptive and coercive is maintaining respect for the moral agency of the client.

Some believe that our job as therapists is to point out the likely consequences of our clients' behavior, basing our observations on scientific data or clinical theory and keeping them free of moral trappings, for which we have no training or competence. In this way of thinking, I would have confined my role in my work with Marcia to that of stating what we know about the negative effects of triangling children into conflicts between ex-spouses. (In my work with the children in family therapy, I would be given leeway to intervene more actively on their behalf, since they would also be my clients—but still not in explicitly moral terms, according to standard therapeutic approaches.) Having served as a neutral clinical consultant in individual therapy, however, my role in the family's decision making would end; I would not weigh in with my private values and moral convictions about what is fair to children. Who am I to say that Marcia's need for authenticity does not outweigh her children's needs for a good relationship with both parents? For explicitly moral discourse, Marcia should talk to her priest.

I have two problems with this argument. First, it is disingenuous. Clients can detect the moral beliefs that underlie a therapist's presentation of "data." If I tell Marcia about the likely negative effects of her actions on her children, Marcia will know that I have personal qualms about her course of action. This discussion is not like one with an auto mechanic who says, "Well, ma'am, if you drive the car too long without checking the oil, you might burn out your engine." There is no moral dimension here: If you are the sole owner of the car, who cares but you if you burn out your engine? Maybe you're ready to junk the car anyway. But such "scientific" discussions with parents carry an implicit "should." I maintain that we should be willing to use more intense moral responses when the clinical circumstances warrant in order to preserve the moral integrity of our clients and to protect vulnerable people from being harmed by our clients' actions.

My second problem with the morality-free approach is that it encourages therapists not to examine their own beliefs, lulling them into the illusory security of thinking they are fully objective. Presumably, Marcia's individual therapist thought he was being neutral and not "moralizing" with her; he was encouraging her to be herself. But he ended up implicitly supporting the morality of individual psychological well-being—interpersonal consequences be damned.

On the other hand, the issues of self-truth and personal authenticity must be accounted for in any morally sensitive therapy. They must not be put in competition with morality in psychotherapy: deciding whether to grow as an agent of one's own life or to be concerned with the well-being of others is not an either-or choice. I will address this issue in the next chapter on truthfulness in therapy.

CHAPTER 4

Truthfulness

I T SEEMED AN INNOCENT-ENOUGH LIE. CHAD'S MOTHER did not approve of his new girlfriend, and Chad, age twenty-one, felt that his mother's underlying agenda was not wanting to be replaced as Chad's first love. He and his mother were recovering from an unhealthy and enmeshed relationship during Chad's adolescence. Chad, who was seeing me for depression, had only recently moved to his own apartment and begun to function emotionally without regular transfusions of support from Mom. With Thanksgiving approaching, Chad wanted to spend the day with his girlfriend and her family instead of with his mother, but he thought that his mother would be hurt and angry if he did not spend Thanksgiving with her. Chad told me he was thinking about telling his mother he had to work all day on Thanksgiving and study that evening for a big exam.

Chad didn't like the idea of lying to his mother, but he also didn't want the grief he would get for abandoning her on a major family holiday. Standard therapeutic discourse would have taken an entirely pragmatic approach, not a moral one, to his decision-making process. What would he accomplish by deceiving his mother, and what would he accomplish by telling her the truth? What was the likelihood of his mother finding out the truth anyway? Was the risk of discovery and recrimination worth the potential gain of avoiding a guilt-inducing discussion? How badly did he want to spend the day with his girlfriend? How upset did he think his mother would be with the straight story, and how uncomfortable might she make it for Chad if he told her the truth?

Another standard therapeutic tack would be to express confidence in Chad's ability to handle the situation without resorting to deception. Chad was cowering before a mother who now had far less power over him than in the past. It would be developmentally healthier for Chad to be aboveboard with his mother and take whatever heat came. He no longer needed to hide his true self.

These two therapeutic stances—the first about the risks and benefits of lying and the second about Chad's self-development and self-assertion—are valid and useful; I called on both stances at various times during my conversation with Chad. I thought it would be better developmentally for Chad to take an open stand, and I thought there was a serious risk that his mother would discover or intuit the truth, leading to even more recriminations than the truth would bring. I explored with Chad why he was afraid to be honest with his mother about the situation and expressed my concern for his personal well-being as he contemplated his decision.

But there was more to our conversation than concerns for Chad's fears and personal well-being. I asked him about the possible effects of the deception on his mother and on his relationship with his mother. The effect on his mother was easy to estimate: if she found out the truth, she would feel hurt and betrayed and patronized, as if Chad felt she could not handle the truth. The effect on the relationship could also be serious: a breach of trust and trustworthiness, and an encouragement to Mom, who had not always been honest with Chad in the past, to weave her own tangled web in the future. In other words, lying ran the risk of hurting his mother and undermining mutual trust in a highly significant relationship.

Mostly I stayed in a low-intensity questioning and exploring mode (responses 1–4) with Chad, only occasionally expressing concern about the consequences for Mom or the relationship. When he looked past his immediate fear of telling his mother the truth, Chad had no trouble seeing these other dimensions. Indeed, it was partly his concern for his mother and their relationship that had led Chad to consult with me. He could see that the first lie ("I'm working and have to study") would probably lead to subsequent lies ("Oh, I had an okay day. We weren't busy at work. I didn't miss the turkey. I only talked briefly to my girlfriend today on the phone"). And Chad's inquiries about his mother's Thanksgiving would feel disingenuous. Witness the distorting power of deception even when the other person does not suspect or has not discovered the deception. As the philosopher Sissela Bok asserts, lies give power to the deceiver over the one deceived, and patterns of lying inevitably distort and erode human relationships, whether or not the deceived person knows it.[1]

After Chad came to the decision to tell his mother the truth—a decision I told him I supported, offering a family therapy session as a venue—I reinforced his image of himself as a courageous, truth-telling individual. In other words, I addressed the theme of integrity. Integrity is harmony between our moral beliefs and our actions. As Chad had grown psychologically healthier in the past few years, he had learned to be more straight and direct with the people in his life. His new forthrightness partly explained why he was uncomfortable with his plan to lie to his mother about Thanksgiving. When he told me he felt much better about facing his mother with the truth, whatever the reaction, I ended my part of the discussion by saying I was glad he had made a choice that was more consistent with his values and beliefs. That is, I emphasized that he was maintaining his moral integrity, which is one of the responsibilities of adulthood, a realm he was just beginning to enter after years of overwhelming emotional dependency. When he shared his decision with his mother in a family therapy session, she took it well and said she was glad her son could be so honest with her.

Chad's story may seem like a fairly benign example of truthfulness, but I chose to present it precisely because his was the kind of situation in which therapists have tended to miss the moral dimension. The effects of deception are much more apparent, and the moral issues therefore much more obvious, when it comes to "big lies"—for example, deception about an affair or about the adoption status of a child. I am interested in exploring the more subtle examples that provide the invisible moral background of routine therapy issues.

Although different, schools of psychotherapy take different approaches to the issue of truthfulness, none deals adequately with the moral dimension. Insight-oriented therapies, beginning with Freud, have emphasized truthfulness with self, that is, discovering and honestly facing hidden or repressed dimensions of one's personality. Humanistic and growth-oriented therapies, beginning with Carl Rogers, have emphasized present self-awareness more than mining for hidden historical and repressed truths about the self, and they add the interpersonal dimension of "speaking my truth" to others. They stress honest expression of wants and feelings, but more for the sake of authenticity and self-development than as a moral mandate. The emphasis is on my need and right to express what is true for me, rather than on your need and right to hear the truth from me.[2] The distinction is not a trivial one.

In Chad's case, the psychodynamically or insight-oriented therapist would have focused on the underlying personality dynamics of Chad's decision about deceiving his mother. Chad's internal process could be viewed as demonstrating his arrested psychological development. The actual choice of lying or truth-telling might be viewed as insignificant; the therapeutic gold would lie in the deeper meaning of his struggle. The question of his mother's needs and rights would not be particularly relevant. My point is not that a psychodynamically oriented therapist would never address the moral dimension of lying, but that the therapeutic discourse generated by the model itself cannot generate moral discussion. Conventionally trained therapists who deal with the moral dimension of life are not using their "native tongue" as therapists; they are making it up as they go along.

Humanistic and growth-oriented therapists working with Chad would have paid more attention to his present decision-making process. One approach would be to help him determine whether he would empower and liberate himself more by telling the truth or by lying to his mother. Operating from the premise that self-expression primarily serves personal needs, the therapist might help Chad do a cost-benefit analysis of the issues, remaining neutral about the outcome as long as it promoted Chad's growth. For example, Chad might decide to not risk harming a relationship he needs by lying. Or the therapist who believes that authentic truth-telling is generally best for individuals might help Chad define his needs clearly in his relationship with his mother. From this perspective, Polonius's admonition to Hamlet, "To thine own self be true," can only be fulfilled if we generally tell our truth to others. In either approach—appealing to personal needs or appealing to personal authenticity—the independent moral claims of others on our trustworthiness are absent.

Two other schools of therapy deserve our attention on the matter of truthfulness. Cognitive-behavioral therapists have a here-and-now orientation to clients' decision making. They focus on uncovering dysfunctional beliefs and developing behavioral skills that will help clients maximize their psychological rewards in life. Cognitive-behavioral therapists might question Chad's catastrophic expectations of what will happen if he tells his mother the truth about his Thanksgiving plans. And they might help him learn the assertiveness skills needed to deal straightforwardly with his mother: the ability to say what he wants and to not be deflected by manipulation. As with the other models of therapy, this approach can be very helpful in a situation like Chad's. But the implicit moral frame is still one of self-interest, even though the therapist might personally hope that Chad ultimately does not think he needs to lie to his mother.[3]

Family therapy is more relational than the individual psychological models of therapy. Most family therapists would be concerned about the effect of Chad's lie on his relationship with his mother. They would advocate for the relationship as well as for Chad. Family therapists would look for the generational patterns of deception and secrets, viewing these as unhealthy for close human connections.[4] However, most family therapists would not conceptualize Chad's dilemma in moral terms, only in relational terms. The implicit moral theory is as follows: people need healthy family relationships, and healthy family relationships are based, in part, on honesty. What is missing in this formulation is the *obligation* family members have to each other. Most family therapists use either the language of health and dysfunction or the language of effective or ineffective problem solving—and sometimes the language of personal empowerment—but they eschew explicit moral discourse about lying. The family therapist Ivan Boszormenyi-Nagy, on the other hand, believes that family members do have responsibilities to one another, because there are moral bonds that connect them.[5] Boszormenyi-Nagy, however, has not written extensively about truthfulness per se. Thus, the family therapy tradition provides some of the important elements of a morality of truthfulness in psychotherapy, although so far it has not gone far enough in elaborating that morality.

Why should therapists care about truthfulness and lying? First, some definitions and conceptual distinctions. By truthfulness, I don't mean always speaking what is factually true; I mean speaking what one *believes* to be true. I tell you that I will come to your party but forget that I have an out-of-town commitment. I was truthful with you, but in error about my ability to follow through.

In other words, there is a distinction between being truthful and speaking the truth. Truthfulness is limited by our self-knowledge and our proclivity for self-deception. But the morality of truthfulness rides on the faithfulness of our words to what we believe.

Belief in one another's truthfulness, according to Sissela Bok, is the cornerstone of social relations, without which cooperation and trust cease to exist. She writes: "Trust in some degree of veracity functions as a *foundation* of relations among human beings; when this trust shatters or wears away, institutions collapse."[6] Therapists should be concerned with truthfulness, then, because it is the foundation of trust, without which human relations disintegrate. Truthfulness is not only about personal insight or personal development or psychological gain; it is also the moral foundation of social relations.

I have been using the term "lie" without defining it. In Sissela Bok's definition, a lie is "an intentionally deceptive message in the form of a statement."[7] I am lying when I assert something I do not believe in order to deceive you. Lying, then, unlike merely hiding from you what I know, is an active process. Chad would not have been lying to his mother if he had said, "I have other plans," and then declined to be specific. He did not necessarily owe his mother a full explanation of his Thanksgiving plans, but he went beyond concealment when he concocted a false story in order to have his mother believe that his intention would have been to spend Thanksgiving at home. Thus, Chad's story would have been a lie as defined here.

Lying, then, is different from keeping secrets, which has to do with the domain of privacy. Everyone, according to Bok, has a legitimate area of privacy, of experiences, thoughts, and wishes that are not to be intruded upon by others. Illegitimate inquiries about one's sexual past are a good example.[8] Truthfulness does not mandate full disclosure of all one's thoughts, actions, and feelings. Given Chad's previous experience with his mother's intrusiveness, if she had inquired about the seriousness of his relationship with his woman friend, he would have been justified in either telling her that he didn't want to get into it or shrugging off her question with an evasive "I don't know." But going beyond maintaining privacy to manufacturing an untrue story would have moved him into the domain of lying, turning the tables on his mother by leading her on. Of course, in everyday life it is not always clear where privacy ends and another person's right to know begins, as when your sexual past has consequences for your current partner's health, or when failing to disclose your deep dissatisfaction with your marriage undermines your spouse's ability to take corrective action or to protect his or her interests. These are delicate areas of moral consultation in therapy.

In addition to undermining relationships, lying imposes unfair and sometimes oppressive burdens on the deceived party. A lie—or, I would add, an unfair secret—often constructs a sense of unreality, a disharmony between observations, feelings, and intuitions, on the one hand, and the "truth" that the other has convinced us to believe, on the other. Rachel Hare-Mustin critiques a published therapy case in which a woman arrived home to confront her partially clothed husband, another woman dressing herself as she emerged from the bathroom, and a rumpled, semen-stained bed. Her husband maintained vehemently that he had a wet dream and that the woman, the girlfriend of a relative, had just stopped to use the bathroom! The wife felt as if she were going crazy. Their marital therapist dealt with this situation as one of two people having different "stories" based on their observations and experiences. Hare-Mustin criticized the therapist's handling of the case on the feminist grounds that he had privileged the oppressive story of the husband over the experience of the wife, who as a woman had been trained to yield to the authority of males.[9]

From the perspective of this chapter, an additional criticism of the case is that the therapist colluded in the husband's lie by treating his story as having equal truth value with the wife's. I am not suggesting that the therapist should have told the husband he was lying—such confrontations rarely accomplish anything—but rather that the therapist should have supported the needs of the wife, who was having trouble resisting the power of a big lie. By not supporting the wife's truth-telling over the husband's lying, the therapist contributed to the distortion of her experience and to the oppressive power of the lie. The therapist fell prey to a kind of postmodern fantasy that all stories are created equal, including those of victims and those of perpetrators. Are the truth claims of historians and Holocaust survivors on an equal footing with the truth claims of those who deny the historicity of the Holocaust? Heaven help us if they are.

I have tried to make the case for truthfulness as a moral issue in psychotherapy, not just as a psychological or interpersonal issue. Next I want to suggest how the two mandates of truthfulness—to be true to oneself and to be morally trustworthy to others—can be linked.

In a very important book entitled *The Ethics of Authenticity*, Charles Taylor sets out to "retrieve" the ideal of personal authenticity from the debasement it has undergone in the last few generations.[10] Taylor proposes that contemporary individualism has an idealistic side as well as a dark side. He begins by describing the principle of modern individualism, which also reads like a declaration of principles for twentieth-century psychotherapy in its myriad forms: "Everyone has a right to develop their own form of life, grounded on their own sense of what is really important or of value. People are called upon to be true to themselves and to seek their own self-fulfillment. What this consists of, each must, in the last instance, determine for him-or-herself. No one else can or should try to dictate its content."[11]

The dark side of individualism has been well documented in recent years. According to Taylor, it is "a centering on the self, which both flattens and narrows our lives, makes them poorer in meaning, and less concerned with others or society."[12] However,

Taylor points out that a moral ideal lurks in the shadows: "The moral ideal behind self-fulfillment is that of being true to oneself, in a specifically modern understanding of that term. . . . Authenticity points us towards a more self-responsible form of life. It allows us to live (potentially) a fuller and more differentiated life, because more fully appropriated as our own."[13] To deny this moral ideal of authenticity is to trash the modern era, which has been so closely linked with individualism, and to reject contemporary psychotherapy as a whole and the reasons so many people seek it.

Taylor wants neither to trash the ideal of authenticity—of being an original person, an agent of your own life and your own values—nor to accept it uncritically. Rather, he argues that a genuine authenticity requires an understanding of how personal identity is formed, namely, through dialogue and human interaction. The dialogical nature of personal identity throughout life means that our relationships define us—they don't just "fulfill" us. Trivialized modes of authenticity define the self atomistically, rendering relationships a means to personal fulfillment. Echoing George Herbert Mead and the symbolic-interactionists, Taylor believes that an instrumental and tentative approach to relationships undermines the very possibility of authenticity, because relationships constitute our identity. They are not coins of the realm to be bartered or kept; they are who we are.

Thus does interpersonal morality enter into the notion of personal authenticity. To be true to myself, I must be true to other people. I have obligations to them because I am one of them and they are part of me. Working out particular moral decisions—do I attend to my needs or to yours?—is often fraught with difficulty, but there is no inherent contradiction between self-fulfillment and moral responsibility to others. This terrifically important idea points to how psychotherapy can retrieve its orienting ethic of self-fulfillment from the debasement it has experienced and provide leadership in promoting a reconciliation between self-fulfillment and moral responsibility in personal relations and community life.

Taylor summarizes his hope for the future in a chapter titled "The Lotta Continua"—the struggle goes on. Rather than rejecting the culture of authenticity as fatally flawed or accepting it as is, "we ought to be trying to persuade people that self-fulfillment, so far from excluding unconditional relationships and moral demands beyond the self, actually requires these in some form. The struggle ought not to be *over* authenticity, for or against, but *about* it, defining its proper meaning. We ought to be trying to lift the culture back up, closer to its motivating ideal."[14]

To demonstrate how difficult these ideals can be on the ground, I will describe a case in which I failed to promote either personal authenticity or interpersonal responsibility to tell the truth.

Nathan, aged fifty-two, called for help with the problem he was having maintaining an erection with his female lover. Although I urged him to invite her to the first session, he declined, saying he wanted to get his "head on straight" first before inviting her in. Thus, my first few sessions were with him alone. His partner eventually did come to therapy, and they were able to restore a reasonably satisfying sexual relationship. A year later Nathan called me back, again asking for an individual appointment. He told me that he had been diagnosed with a kidney condition that was limiting his generally boundless energy and that would almost certainly limit his life expectancy, though the doctors could not say by how much. He was also having relationship troubles with his partner, to whom he was now married. He had not told her about the seriousness of his condition; in fact, he had told her that he had a fairly benign problem that could be controlled with medication.

When I raised a concern about Nathan not telling his wife the truth about his condition, he became agitated, telling me that she could not handle the truth. It would upset her too much and make her too insecure about the future. I suggested that perhaps he was responding to his own fears and his natural desire to protect her, rather than to her inability to handle the information. (I knew her to be a strong woman who had dealt with a number of painful situations in her life.) I reiterated my concern about not telling her the truth: she shared the same metaphorical lifeboat with him and needed to know what was going on with her partner.

Nathan pleaded with me not to tell her. I replied that it was not my place to tell her anything but that I was concerned about him not telling her. Then he asked me, in fact insisted, that I not require him to tell her as a condition of our subsequent couples therapy. He bought time with me by saying he had to work out his own way of telling her and could not do it right away. I reluctantly, and I think mistakenly, agreed to let the matter rest for the time being. From then on, my hands were tied in the marital therapy because I knew a secret the wife did not know and because I knew he had lied to her about his health. He wielded a form of informational power over her, and I collaborated.

I think I was lured into the mistake because the issue was his personal health and he had the legal right to keep his diagnosis private. I certainly did not have the right to disclose it for him. What I did not see at the time was that by engaging in marital therapy under these conditions, I was endorsing his decision to maintain the lie and supporting the illusion that his wife's future was reasonably secure, that there was no leak in their lifeboat. I bit the bait of "I'll get there, I'll tell her eventually." Nathan had no intention of telling her, I had no plan for dealing with the issue, and I ended up supporting his lie. For this and other reasons not related to truthfulness, the therapy was not successful.

What do I wish I had done with Nathan? I wish I had used moral response number 8: decline to see him with his wife in marital therapy because I could not support his lying to her about his health problem. I certainly would have been willing to continue with him in individual therapy and would have continued to broach the issue of leveling with his wife, including dealing with his anger at me for not cooperating. In other words, I do not require my clients to be virtuous in order to continue in therapy.

There would be few clients and few therapists if the standard of full moral integrity was imposed on all of us. But I cannot witness lies that harm or disenfranchise other people without the understanding that I can bring the matter to the therapeutic conversation. The problem with my doing couples therapy with Nathan and his wife was that I had promised not to bring the matter up in front of her. Based on deception, the therapy was doomed, and I had compromised myself ethically as a therapist for the wife and the husband alike.

Nathan's lie was a big one. But what about so-called white lies? White lies can be defined as those intended to avoid social embarrassment. Although Sissela Bok believes that white lies should be avoided because they eventually undermine trust in a person's veracity,[15] it is valid to make a distinction between a white lie that attempts to save another person social embarrassment and one that is intended to protect yourself from being embarrassed by your own social missteps.

An example of a "sensitive" white lie is your response when your great-aunt asks you how you like the (ugly) sweater she knitted for your birthday. A benign and caring white lie is likely to follow: "It was very nice, Aunt Mary. Thank you." Adding that it's the best sweater you ever owned—well, that's crossing over the line into the territory of a deceptive, self-serving lie. Simply telling someone that you like a gift is the social equivalent of saying "Fine" when someone asks how you are. To be fully honest ("I really don't care for the color or the texture") would be cruel, and to equivocate ("Yes, it's a sweater all right") would be mocking.

The second category of white lies, saving face for yourself, is more problematic. A couple I had been seeing for marital therapy—Stan and Hope—eventually got around to discussing their differences in raising their teenagers. One of their differences related to the virtue of truthfulness versus encouraging white lies and other small deceptions. They gave a recent example. Nineteen-year-old Kristen, in her first year at a local private college, was to represent the first-year students at a function for parents sponsored by the board of trustees. Not realizing that this was a fairly formal activity, she showed up in jeans and a sweatshirt. Embarrassed, she asked her mother for advice. Hope suggested that, when it came time to speak to the group, Kristen tell the audience that she had been volunteering that afternoon in a homeless shelter and did not have time to change clothes before coming to give her speech. It worked perfectly. The parents and administrators in the audience murmured their understanding and appreciation, and Kristen's speech was a big success. In fact, she did volunteer regularly at a homeless shelter and was a good all-around student and citizen, but that day she had miscalculated the dress code, not the timing of her volunteer commitment versus her speaking commitment. She lied to avoid social embarrassment.

Hope had no problem with her advice and what her daughter had done. Stan felt uncomfortable but could not articulate his concerns well. Hope asked, "Who was harmed?" It was a small white lie in her view. No one was hurt or even inconvenienced, and Kristen was spared discomfort from an honest mistake. This disagreement was not a big issue in the couple's relationship; they had worked through far more difficult marital issues and were currently in a collaborative relationship mode. But they were curious about my reaction, and I felt I could give them a parenting "consultation" without excessive danger of being triangled into a marital conflict.

I began by expressing my understanding of their desire to protect their children from social embarrassment, especially in a situation in which their daughter had prepared well but miscalculated in a way that could have ruined the occasion for her. And I expressed support for their overall approach to parenting their children, who seemed to be growing up as responsible and sensitive people. But I went on to express my concern about the message that it is okay to play with the truth to avoid the social consequences of your actions. I said I was worried about their children's sense of truthfulness and integrity if they got into the habit of stopping to calculate whether to make up a story to cover their mistakes. I wondered whether Hope and Stan would find their children trustworthy as adults when they offered excuses for declining their parents' invitations to dinner. Would "I have to work late" be the truth or a convenient white lie to disguise a disinclination to visit?

In my view, evading embarrassment and minor hassles through the use of white lies is a form of moral cowardice that undermines personal character and trustworthiness in human relationships. I know a professional person whose white lies in the past have evoked suspicion about his excuses in the present; for instance, people have checked to see if the trains were actually delayed on the day he excused his lateness because of a late train.

What should a therapist's stance be toward clients' white lies? I often take the posture of gently challenging these deceptions when clients bring them up. I may ask what is leading the client to be fearful about being up front. For example, Elliott did not want to trade child-care weekends with his ex-wife, but he also did not want to tell her his plans for that weekend. Instead of saying, "I can't do it," or, "I have other plans," he was going to tell her that he had to work that weekend. Why? Because he did not want to deal with her questions about why he didn't want to trade weekends. A conflict avoider in his marriage, he continued to reflexively duck conflict, preferring to give a false explanation that his ex-wife could not contest.

I helped Elliott see that he was strong enough to stand up to his ex-wife without making up excuses for his actions. His white lie was part of older behavior patterns that had hurt him and his marriage in the past, patterns that he was unlearning. I suspected that his wife often played along, pretending to believe Elliott's excuses but accumulating "deception credits" for the next round of indirect conflict, when she could lie to him. The first level I worked on, then, was the psychological and interpersonal level: Elliott needed to learn to be assertive with his ex-wife and not let himself be manipulated or intimidated by her demandingness.

After Elliott shored up his resolve to be direct with his ex-wife—a decision he clearly felt better about than he would have about hiding through a lie—I moved the discussion briefly to the moral level. I told Elliott that I was glad he had decided to act in a way that was consistent with how I saw him approaching life in other areas: as an honest man who said what he believed. I said I would hate to see him compromise himself to avoid being hassled by his ex-wife. In this way, I was supporting his sense of moral integrity as a truthful person.

In the case of Hope and Stan and their daughter's white lie, the couple ended up not agreeing with me and told me so. They saw their own and their children's white lies as trivial and, in fact, as a sophisticated way to handle social difficulties. Our disagreement was respectful. Having offered my consultation, I let the matter go, while filing away my perspective and concern for possible future use in the therapy.

A good guideline for moral consultation in psychotherapy: if a client always ends up agreeing with the therapist, the therapist is probably doing something wrong—being coercive, shaming, or unaware of the client's need to please.

When I told Elliott that I saw him as an honest man, I was being truthful. Elliott was a group therapy member who could be counted on to say what he was seeing and hearing. In the wonderful phrase I learned when I lived in Oklahoma, he would "put the snake on the table." He generally possessed the virtue of truthfulness, a quality he sometimes compromised, however, to avoid short-term pain with his ex-wife. My point in saying that I believed what I said about him is that therapists cannot adequately support the virtue of truthfulness in our clients unless we practice it ourselves in therapy. If I had told Elliott I saw him as honest when I did not see him that way, then I would have been lying to him to help him be truthful—a destructive paradox if there ever was one.[16]

If we believe that truthfulness is the bedrock of trust in interpersonal relations for our clients, then we should see it the same way in our own conduct with clients. Telling Elliott something I did not believe, for the purpose of encouraging him to make changes, would have been wrong ethically. I am speaking narrowly here of "self-disbelieved" statements that deceive the client about our real beliefs. Social mores used to permit physicians to tell white lies out of paternalistic concern for the patient's well-being. But we no longer tolerate their assuming the power to tell us we have some vague "liver disease" when we actually have liver cancer. Bending the truth is no longer acceptable in psychotherapists as well.

I don't know how widespread the practice of deception by therapists is, but every therapist has heard examples. I know a therapist who sometimes tells parents he has children the ages of their children. This builds confidence in his expertise, he believes. I know a therapist who sometimes tells clients she has consulted with expert colleagues about their case when she has not. In each example, the therapist lies for the good of the client, but at great peril to the trustworthiness of the clinical relationship—and, I believe, to the integrity of the therapist.

Even more suspect are white lies that are clearly intended to serve the therapist's purposes more than the client's. Some therapists, upon arriving late for their first session of the morning or after lunch, routinely say that traffic held them up when in fact they overslept or dawdled over lunch with a friend. A colleague of mine recounted saying this at the beginning of a cotherapy session and then experiencing the distortion within himself at having lied to the clients. He finally corrected his misstatement and offered to reduce the fee if the clients wanted. (They had begun the session with the cotherapist and were paying fees for each therapist separately.) Some might consider his action morally scrupulous and clinically risky, but he spoke up to salvage his ability to be fully trustworthy with his clients.

In discussing deception by therapists, it is important to keep in mind the distinction between a lie told as an intentionally deceptive statement and a therapist's attempt to partially conceal his or her beliefs for a time in therapy. Timing is at the heart of the art of therapy. I may believe after the first thirty minutes with my client that she is much too emotionally involved with her daughter, and that this emotional enmeshment is contributing to her daughter's problems. But I am not obligated to spell out this belief at the beginning of therapy, when such a suggestion might overwhelm her with guilt and shame—and send her looking elsewhere for a more compassionate therapist. Unlike medical physicians, therapists must be given leeway to time their observations according to the client's readiness to hear them. A certain amount of concealment, then, is necessary during the process of therapy. In my experience, however, successful therapy almost invariably involves my full disclosure, with care and sensitivity, of my beliefs about the client's issues.

Similarly, I see nothing unethical about a therapist choosing to emphasize one aspect of his or her beliefs. If my client is convinced that a problem stems from lack of self-esteem, then I can ethically emphasize this problem in initially framing the issues, even though I may think other issues are more fundamental. In the complex mosaic of explanations for human problems, there are plenty of issues therapists can choose to emphasize at different points in therapy. The moral problem only occurs when the therapist asserts something he or she does not believe to be true at all. For example, I would not pretend to believe astrological explanations even if I thought the client would connect with me better in therapy.

In the same way, the use of metaphor and story does not violate the ethic of truthfulness as long as the client understands that the therapist is speaking in indirect, symbolic terms. The family therapist Carl Whitaker is known for making outlandish statements, such as, "I think you should ditch your wife and marry your mother." Clients presumably realize that he is speaking in provocative metaphor here, not making a literal suggestion about a course of action. The moral danger, then, lies in deceiving clients. The trap for therapists is the desire to be "effective," to bring about change by means of benevolent deception. Therapeutic white lies, however, corrode the foundations of our clinical relationships and violate the right of clients to be spared deception by those they trust.

Lying is about power and covert self-protection, and truthfulness (within the context of sensitivity) is about sharing power and about the willingness to be vulnerable. Ultimately, there is no contradiction between truthfulness as a hallmark of personal authenticity and empowerment and truthfulness as a moral mandate. All the traditional theories of individual psychotherapy support the value of truthfulness for the well-being of individuals. What they miss is that truthfulness is important in the moral order of relations between people—the notion that others have legitimate demands on us for honesty—and that truthfulness is a core element of character. If a therapist fails to see the moral dimension of being truthful, then he or she will help clients speak the truth only when it serves their needs or promotes their personal growth. And such therapists may resort to their own mental calculus about truthfulness and deception in and out of therapy. In either case, the bent needle of truthfulness can only knit a tangled relational web.

CHAPTER 5

Community

FOR MANY PEOPLE, PSYCHOTHERAPY HAS REPLACED FAMILY as the only reliable haven in a heartless world. In fact, psychotherapy is where people turn to be healed from the hurts they believe their families inflicted on them. Therapy is the ultimate private experience, occurring in small spaces bounded by thick walls of confidentiality. As ministers of this most intimate ritual, therapists generally keep the discourse personal, focusing on the client's feelings and thoughts and close relationships. Talk about the outside world of community and its institutions distracts from the traditional goals of therapy unless it can be turned into greater understanding of individual or family dynamics.

This private hearth of psychotherapy is somehow terribly constricting, as the following case illustrates. Anna and Don, both in their midthirties, had a son with cystic fibrosis and a daughter with congenital neurological defects. Overwhelmed by years of caregiving for these children, Anna had sought out psychotherapy several times over the years, with mixed results. She had a number of personal problems, including a familial tendency toward depression and low self-esteem, but her major complaints concerned her tortuous relationships with the myriad physicians in

her children's lives and her struggles to obtain medical and reha-
bilitative benefits from the health care system. She did not com-
plain about the division of marital labor: Don worked very hard to
maintain a job that had good medical benefits and Anna devoted
her energies to the children and, increasingly, to giving talks to
parents and health professionals about managing cystic fibrosis
and childhood disabilities.

Two crucial aspects of this case—the impact of the health care
system on Anna and her family, and Anna's growing desire to
change the system—were never part of her prior therapy except as
venues for understanding her personal problems. Her struggles
with the medical team were interpreted as reflecting her difficulty
with interpersonal boundaries (partly true). Her busyness from
giving talks and workshops was interpreted as a misplaced effort
to heal herself. (Partly true, perhaps, but why dismiss her efforts?)
Nowhere was the community dimension of the problem acknowledged, and nowhere were her efforts to change the community
honored. I might add that Anna had seen very good therapists
who responded no differently than I would have for most of my
career. The issue is not competence but paradigm.

When I saw Anna and Don in therapy, I talked with them
about their relationships with health professionals. I saw how the
medical specialists were relying on Anna's knowledge of the children's medical conditions to encourage her to play the role of pediatric nurse practitioner instead of mother. But when she tried to
initiate communication or express opinions in the manner of a
pediatric nurse practitioner, the physicians saw her as overinvolved and intruding on their medical responsibility. She was
given too much responsibility for her children's medical care, but
punished when she exercised it. I also saw how Don's peripheral
position in these clinical relationships made it more difficult for
her to negotiate changes, because the medical team personalized
its conflicts with her by attributing them to her psychological
problems.

When there is a chronic illness in a family, that family has a chronic relationship with the health care system, and the effects of that system can be as pervasive as those of other family members.[1] As a result of our discussions in therapy, Anna could acknowledge her contributions to the problems but no longer felt totally responsible. We were able to work out a plan of personal and family change and held meetings with the health care team to create a better balance of responsibility and respect. This outcome reflected the advantage of understanding a client's problems in community terms. I return to this case later in the chapter to illustrate a second point about clients giving back to their communities.

When a therapist turns the focus to community forces and institutions—such as racism, sexism, poverty, health care systems, schools, social service systems, and workplaces—the client's personal and family issues need not be neglected. A community-oriented focus is an acknowledgment that clients and their families should not be assigned primary responsibility for problems stemming from forces in their environment. A poor, African-American single mother, for example, must cope with problems partly attributable to institutional racism and institutional sexism; helping her see her problems in the larger context can help her avoid paralyzing self-blame.

Paying attention to community forces is not new to social work or to sociology or to the pioneers in community mental health, but unfortunately, it is new to mainstream psychotherapy, whose explanations for human problems have centered on individuals, sometimes expanding only so far as to include families. We have been trained to use microscopes, which make the heavens invisible. However, in recent years, innovative therapists, spurred by the traditions of multiculturalism and feminism, have begun to pay more systematic attention to the social, institutional, and political forces affecting individuals and families.[2]

In a powerful article on middle-class African-American men in therapy, Anderson Franklin wrote about the pileup of social indignities many black men experience in their daily lives—cabs passing them by, restaurant checks handed to their white colleagues, fearful looks from fellow passengers on elevators—along with larger discriminations such as restricted work assignments that carry less opportunity. Franklin described how some therapists take the status quo as a given and focus on challenging the client to cope more constructively with it. In some circles, this might be considered good reality-based therapy: you can't change cab drivers and waiters, so why get worked up over it? This sanitized therapeutic discourse, however, robs human experience of its moral fervor. Outrage about injustice in society has an important place in psychotherapy.[3]

Over the past two decades, feminist therapists have also led the way in showing how intertwined are the personal and the political in human life. They have deconstructed powerful images, such as the overinvolved, pathogenic mother, and revealed the layers of contradiction created for women in society: motherhood is your mission and your identity, but if you work too hard at it you will be blamed for all manner of problems your children develop. Feminist therapists have shown how lack of equal opportunity for women in the work force is reflected in power differentials between women and men in the family. And feminist therapists have developed ways to help clients take effective action to change their families and the world around them, for example, in resisting domestic violence, instead of staying focused on personal failure to cope with an unfair world.[4]

When working with Anna and Don, I validated Anna's belief that her family was being treated unfairly by the medical team, and that she especially was expected as a mother to do too much—and then was being scapegoated for becoming overinvolved. After talking with the physicians, I concluded that no one was willing to take responsibility for the kind of coordination required to take Anna out of her nurse practitioner role and allow her to be a mother. The primary care physician, who would have been the appropriate coordinator for the children's care, said she was "too busy" to keep up on such a complicated case involving so many subspecialists. And nobody else stepped into the breach. I concluded that the medical team was being underresponsible and unfair to this family, and I said this to the parents, who had been sensing the injustice all along. I tried to say these things, however, without expressing animosity toward the medical team or scapegoating them for problems that partly stemmed from the way health care is organized in this country.

Despite the absence of personal villains, this case was not simply a matter of poor communication or inadequate case management; it evinced a lack of commitment to the welfare of the children and the family, and an exploitative set of expectations of the mother. What made this situation chronically dysfunctional was that the primary care physician was not willing to say, "I can't do it," and relinquish responsibility for the case. She hung on, blaming the mother for screwups. Finally, the family moved the children's care to different providers who offered a fair division of responsibility between the medical team and the family. I believe that this step of empowerment did more for Anna's emotional health than the years of looking inward at herself, although that personal work may have prepared her for what she had to do.

I want to make it clear again that I am not proposing an either-or approach to therapy—either private issues or community issues. Anderson Franklin underlines the importance of helping oppressed clients distinguish between the effects of oppression and their own contributions to their problems.[5] A community-sensitive therapy carries the danger of treating clients like helpless victims of social forces beyond their influence or control, thereby robbing them of their own moral agency. Being shafted at work does not bestow permission to be mean-spirited at home, although understanding the connections between the two can help. The challenge is to embrace the private discourse of the psychological and interpersonal realm along with the public discourse of the social and political realm, without reducing either to the other and without editing out the moral domain. This is no small task for therapists in a mental health world increasingly oriented to narrow diagnoses and treatment plans.

Morality, then, is not just a personal matter; it is a community matter as well. Simply stated, communities and community institutions have bonds of moral obligation to individuals and families. Social institutions—schools, churches, government at all levels, the marketplace, the health and social service systems—constitute what Robert Bellah and his colleagues termed the "moral ecology" of individual and family life.[6] Social institutions' primary moral obligation is ensuring justice—providing fair and equal opportunities and resources to all members of the community. When social institutions are unjust, widespread individual, family, and community alienation and breakdown are inevitable. This connection between private and public morality is missed by many who emphasize "family values" without simultaneously scrutinizing the values practiced by societal institutions.

The ecology of modern social institutions has been categorized by social scientists into three domains: the market, the state, and the civil society. The market is the world of economics and free enterprise. Its reigning ideals are rational choice, efficiency, and flexibility. Its chief moral principle is that we are obligated primarily to ourselves; the rational pursuit of self-interest will benefit the society collectively. The modern democratic state, on the other hand, embraces ideals of collective obligation, egalitarianism, intergroup politics, and external authority. Leaders of modern nation-states prefer to avoid the language of morality; instead, they focus on mediating between interest groups, attempting cost-efficient collective responses to economic and social problems, and using laws to limit the excesses of the market and the self-interest of individuals.[7]

The "civil society" refers to the private sector situated between the market and the state. The term has been used in different ways since the time of David Hume, but it generally refers to families, local groups, neighborhoods, friendship networks, personal work-place ties, volunteer organizations, churches, and various sponta-neous groups and movements.[8] Participation in domains of the civil society is voluntary in a way that being a market consumer or a citizen is not voluntary; you can choose whether to join a church or the Elks Club or a stop-the-violence association. The ideals of the civil society, according to Alan Wolfe, are trust, solidarity, and mutual obligation. The civil society is where individuals find their deepest sense of connection and where the social construction of morality occurs in everyday life. What we think of as strong com-munities have rich layers of private, voluntary organizations and associations that counterbalance the profit motive of the market and the bureaucratic legalisms of the government. However, the strength of the civil society (especially in the United States) is receding rapidly before the forces of the market and the state.[9] In many ways, the breakdown of community in the United States and in the Western world is the breakdown of civil society.

Alan Wolfe describes the underlying similarity between the market and the state as they have assumed more preeminence in defining the moral bonds that traditionally were the focus of the civil society:

> Although there are obvious and important differences between the market and the state, they also share similar logics, which is why ... they often have similar results. Neither speaks well of obliga-tions to other people simply as people, treating them instead as cit-izens or as opportunities. Neither puts its emphasis on the bonds that tie people together because they want to be tied together with-out regard for their immediate self-interest or for some external authority having the power to enforce those ties. Finally—and the point I want to emphasize most in [this book]—neither wishes to recognize one of the very things that make liberal [democracies]

modern: that people are capable of participating in the making of their own moral rules.[10]

How does this sociological discussion apply to the work of psychotherapists? I believe that the shrinking influence of the civil society (which I use interchangeably with the more evocative term "family and community" in the following discussion) in the face of the juggernaut of market and state is the major social factor in the widespread use of psychotherapy in the late twentieth century. In other words, the more the family and the community deteriorate, the more business we have as therapists. The rates of major depression, for example, have increased with every generation in the past fifty years throughout most nations of the world as they have gone through urbanization and the fragmentation of communities.[11] Individuals are increasingly experiencing what the sociologist Emile Durkheim began to detect a hundred years ago: the atomization of society, which produces alienated individuals bereft of clear norms for guiding their behavior.[12] Therapists' caseloads are filled with individuals who are weakly moored to family and community and who find less and less personal meaning in their roles as consumers and citizens—the two major roles offered by the market and the state. Psychotherapy has become the doctor of the rootless modern soul.

Unfortunately, instead of decrying this change and calling for renewal of family and community, the field of psychotherapy has accepted—and sometimes indirectly promoted—the premise that the erosion of the power of the civil society is necessary to free the individual to pursue personal authenticity and psychological gain. We do help clients achieve better "relationships," but with an emphasis on voluntary, mutually satisfying connections that lack a sense of obligation and responsibility for one another's welfare. When this type of relationship becomes the norm, the ethic of the market has enveloped the private domain in its acquisitive grasp.[13]

In part, liberation from the civil society has been useful and necessary for modern men and women. The world of family and community is susceptible to its own forms of oppression, as seen in domestic violence, racial segregation, and community pressures to continue agricultural practices that hurt the land.[14] Because most civil societies of the past did not recognize women and minorities as full participants, the freedom espoused by the state and the market is essential in a modern democratic society. We cannot go back to the family or community of nostalgia, nor would most of us want to if we could. But as Alan Wolfe maintains, what used to be a three-way dialogue of mutual restraint—among market, state, and civil society—has become a two-way dialogue. Instead of the moral sensibilities of family and community setting limits on the self-interest of the market and the impersonality and authoritarianism of the state, these two domains have increasingly penetrated the heart of family and community—with the unwitting assistance of psychotherapists, I might add.

The clearest indication of how psychotherapists have distrusted the civil society can be found in the almost complete silence in the psychotherapy literature on the issue of clients' responsibilities for, and obligations to, their communities. Here we are faced with an even more fundamental challenge to the traditional psychotherapy paradigm than the moral ecology approach described above. As important as it is for therapists to be ecological in their work—to take into account the influence of social forces and institutions on clients' lives and problems—the direction of influence and responsibility is still outward to inward, the community's influence on the individual or family, not vice versa. The new writing on the social and political contexts of psychotherapy deals nearly exclusively with helping clients make a life for themselves in the face of toxic community forces. Social activism, when it is discussed, takes the form of advocating for one's legitimate rights in the community.

. Simply stated, we have learned that communities have responsibilities for the welfare of individuals. But what about individuals' responsibilities to promote the welfare of their communities, to make them safer, more humane, more beautiful, more just? On this issue of what Thomas Jefferson called "civic friendship," psychotherapy has been nearly mute for a century.

Encouraging new voices of social responsibility are beginning to emerge in psychotherapy, the voices of writers who combine rights within communities with obligations toward communities. Mary Nicholas writes about the importance of altruism toward one's community, a quality she notes has often been pathologized in the past.[15] Andrew Samuels sets out to break down the boundaries between politics and psychology and calls for a "new psychological valuing of the potential of political engagement itself."[16] James Hillman and Michael Ventura, in *We've Had a Hundred Years of Psychotherapy—and the World's Getting Worse*, argue that the dominant models of psychotherapy have contributed to the breakdown of human community by ignoring the social and political domains and celebrating the private and personal domains. They write: "There is a decline in political sense. No sensitivity to the real issues. Why are the intelligent people—at least among the white middle class—so passive now? Why? Because the sensitive, intelligent people are in therapy! They've been in therapy in the United States for 30, 40 years, and during that time there's been a tremendous political decline in this country."[17]

Although therapists do not tell clients to be politically passive, I see many therapists negatively interpreting their clients' public-service sensibilities and activities. One of Anna's therapists suggested that she was not so much serving other families through her teaching as trying vicariously to heal her own family. A friend told me of his meeting with a therapist just before he departed for Northern Ireland to work with war-oppressed children in the early 1970s. The therapist suggested that my friend was doing this work to deal with the internal war of his own childhood. A colleague curtailed her social activism after her therapist reframed it as a misguided effort to fill a hole inside herself by trying to save the world.

I have heard these stories continually since I began speaking with other professionals about community commitment and began honoring these commitments among my clients. I met a social activist who builds community and focuses attention on social and environmental issues by means of community involvement projects. He has been told by two personal therapists, as well as by the many therapists in his friendship circle—liberals all!— that his social activism stems from unfinished personal business. When he takes care of his personal business, so the line goes, he will stop acting out his missionary zeal in the world.

θ works all things for good.

All of these socially committed individuals appreciate that their personal issues are involved in their choice of work—as they are for all of us, including therapists. But they understandably resent being patronized and pathologized for their energetic work to make a difference in promoting the civil society. When clients tell us they want to change the world, we see them as cosmically co-dependent. A stint of good psychotherapy will send them back to their private world where they can criticize "society" without doing anything about it.

What about those who are heroically committed to community service? We tend not to see them in therapy. A book by the developmental psychologists Anne Colby and William Damon gives a fascinating recounting of the lives of five moral exemplars in the United States, persons cited by a wide range of acquaintances for their vast vision and personal dedication to serving disenfranchised people. Although not unable to be introspective, these individuals were busy activists and not especially focused on their own needs or psychological conflicts. Each was making an important difference in a local community.[18] As I finished the book, I felt a wave of relief that these servants of humanity had not fallen into the clutches of psychotherapists, including me not so many years ago.

Although Hillman and Ventura do a fine job of provocatively raising the issue of therapy's often discouraging effect on clients' sense of public responsibility, they oversimplify in suggesting that without so many people in psychotherapy the political world would be better off. Psychotherapy is just one social institution caught up in a "habit of the heart" in contemporary America that focuses on private gain over public good. If we did not have psychotherapy, more people would play casinos or broker junk bonds. The problem is that psychotherapists, who tend to view themselves as countercultural in promoting humanistic values, are actually as mainstream as the chamber of commerce in promoting a private-public split.

The toughest issue is one that Hillman and Ventura don't take on directly: how to translate into sensitive clinical practice the idea that clients have responsibilities to their communities. People come to us because they are in pain and want personal help for themselves and their families, not because they are looking for a social cause. Sometimes clients are so immobilized that all they can do is take care of their immediate crisis. The last thing they need is a lecture on social responsibility or a list of volunteer community service projects from which to choose before the next session. As in all things clinical, timing is critical, and the needs of our clients cannot be sacrificed to our own agendas for social change.

The problem with this traditional way of prioritizing private pain over public involvement, however, is that its vision is too narrow. There is no fundamental contradiction between pursuing personal needs and promoting the welfare of the community. Therefore, when we promote clients' positive involvement in community, we promote their own well-being as well. I am not proposing a new prescription for social activism so much as a new description of the seamless web that connects private good and public good. We are like fish in the ocean: our personal well-being is tied inexorably to our natural and social environment. Like responsible parenting, responsible participation in activities to preserve and promote that environment is at once generous and self-serving. This does not mean that all community service can be reduced to the motive of self-interest, but that self-interest is embraced and transcended in an ethic of the common good.

Responsible involvement with the larger world is necessary for what Charles Taylor calls the "horizon of significance" that gives meaning to human life and human actions. Turning inward to a private cocoon of self and close relationships is ultimately self-defeating because it robs life of larger meaning. It is also self-defeating because, as Alexis de Tocqueville warned over 150 years ago, a society in which individuals are "enclosed in their own hearts" is one in which government will become increasingly powerful in a "soft" despotism fueled by citizens' lack of interest in self-government and political culture.[19]

Taylor summarizes the connection between personal meaning and larger concerns:

> The agent seeking significance in life, trying to define him- or herself meaningfully, has to exist in a horizon of important questions. This is what is self-defeating in modes of contemporary culture that concentrate on self-fulfillment in *opposition* to the demands of society, or nature, which *shut out* history and the bonds of solidarity.... Otherwise put, I can define my identity only against the background of things that matter. But to bracket out history, nature, society, the demands of solidarity, would be to eliminate all candidates for what matters. Only if I exist in a world in which history, or the demands of nature, or the needs of my fellow human beings, or the duties of citizenship, or the call of God, or something else of this order *matters* crucially, can I define an identity for myself that is not trivial. Authenticity is not the enemy of demands that emanate from beyond the self; it supposes such demands.[20]

Once we accept the life-enhancing connection between the private and the public, between what feminists call the personal and the political, the matter of explicit dialogue in therapy becomes somewhat less problematical. As with moral issues in general, the clearest opportunity for discussing community issues occurs when clients bring them up. The psychologist Richard Sherman has observed that clients often mention world and national concerns at the beginning of therapy sessions, in the greeting and getting-settled phase of the hour. He points out that therapists usually treat these discussions as chitchat, not as grist for the therapeutic mill.[21] What is said is rarely integrated into the substance of therapy.

In the early 1990s, when the Persian Gulf War loomed so large in America's consciousness for many months, a number of my clients mentioned the war spontaneously during the initial phase of therapy sessions. Sometimes I brought it up myself in the form of a question such as, "Are you following the Persian Gulf situation these days?" Some clients talked about how they were dealing with their own and their children's questions and anxieties. Not infrequently, we had a brief conversation about the client's sense of the rightness of our government's action. In several marital therapy cases, I brought up the Gulf War during the middle of a session as a way of pointing out how conflict escalates at every social level from the couple to nation-states.

These discussions of the war were never lengthy, but neither were they on the order of ordinary chitchat about Minnesota weather. I was inquiring not only about how the war was affecting my clients but also—and this is the crucial point for this chapter—about how my clients felt about the war as citizens of a warring country. I was affirming them—and myself—as concerned members of a nation and of the world community. I was impressed with how some of my clients applied the systems ideas they had learned in therapy to their understanding of the international conflict. Not everyone reached the same conclusions, of course, about what our country should have been doing, and I did not recommend what actions my clients should take. But after one client said she was going to call her senator, I told her that I had called that morning and had the phone number if she wanted it. She took it.

Is this an inappropriate intrusion of politics into the private world of therapy? Was I imposing my values in bringing up the war and especially in passing on the senator's phone number? From my perspective, to be silent about the major international conflict of the day would have been like ignoring the elephant in the room. And to not respect my clients' concerns and beliefs about the war would have been treating them like children. As adults, we carry civic responsibilities to participate in the process of public discussion and debate. Why should these issues be deleted from therapeutic discourse?

Moving from the international to the local, consider the case of Byron, a pediatrician who had contributed mightily to children's health care in his community over a long and distinguished career. He saw me after his wife left him. He expressed regret that his heavy commitment to his work had rendered him emotionally unavailable in his marriage, although he had remained in good emotional contact with his children, who were now adults. Previous individual therapy had left Byron with the belief that his work served primarily as his escape from dealing honestly with his problems at home and as a refuge where he could control his environment and get his emotional needs met by patients, families, and staff. He spoke of his work commitment with self-reproach, despite acknowledging that he had done some good things along the way.

How sad, I thought, that this man has been taught by therapists to trivialize his contributions to his community. Through his efforts, health care for children in his community was far better. He had declined more lucrative jobs in order to effect programmatic changes in a local hospital. He had mentored scores of younger pediatricians, and he had promoted public health initiatives. And yet he had been initiated into a myopic therapeutic worldview that ignored or disparaged these contributions to the common good because he had not developed his inner emotional world sufficiently and had settled for a lifeless marriage. Yes, he had plenty to work on in these areas, but these personal limitations did not vitiate a lifetime of service.

In my conversation with Byron, I gently challenged his self-deprecating remarks about his work. I encouraged him to talk about what he had accomplished, noting afterward that his was a story of significant contributions to the welfare of children, families, and the community. Instead of denigrating his civic friendship, I honored it. Byron needed more balance between his inner and outer worlds, but he did not have to be ashamed of his professional dedication. Therapists, I fear, have such a strong bias toward the intimate world that they ignore or disparage the community world, rather than taking the simple but powerful stance of acknowledging and affirming clients' values and commitments—the first and most basic form of moral discourse.

Sometimes clients directly bring up their community-serving activities, such as running a religious education program, serving on boards, volunteering at a school, or working at a food bank. Sometimes they are involved in social action at even larger levels, such as working on global environmental issues. When clients bring up these involvements, therapists tend to respond in terms of how the activity serves the needs and goals of the client. If the therapist thinks the involvement is "healthy" for the client, then the therapist may inquire about the psychological benefits it offers. There is nothing wrong about this kind of discussion; the best sustained commitments are those that benefit the giver and the receiver. But what is missing is explicit acknowledgment of the client's contributions to the welfare of others in the community. Helping children learn at school, providing leadership for community boards, feeding the homeless—these are morally praiseworthy activities because they do good for others. They build the civil society outside of the profit motive and legislated government programs. They are forms of civic friendship.

Many therapists have the same cynicism that journalists do in evaluating the motives of public officials and prominent business leaders who espouse altruistic initiatives. How many times have you heard a therapist assert that only a disturbed personality (narcissistic, antisocial, or some other breed) would run for higher office? With this type of cynical brush stroke, we dismiss the possibility that community leaders could have ideals for community service in addition to their desire for power or profit.

I don't want to sound naive here. Like any other important human effort, such as caring for one's children, altruistic activities can be done for primarily self-serving reasons. You can volunteer at a community program in order to land a job there—not an immoral reason to be sure, but not one stemming from the virtue of community service. I worked with an alcoholic man who had served on the county alcoholism council for years; his volunteering was more an act of self-deception than of civic commitment. But when a client's service to the community appears to stem from both self-service and altruism, then we should support both sides of the client's experience—not only as it helps the client grow personally but also as it enables the client to help others in the community.

I know a hunger activist who was told by her therapist that she was trying to fill a hole inside herself by "feeding" the world. It was only after "graduating" from therapy that she felt free to give herself over to her mission and make a truly international contribution. I wonder how many people with strong religious convictions underlying their community service keep these motives hidden in therapy for fear that the therapist will find a bona fide psychological problem underlying their conscious religious motivations. Even if there are psychological problems present, my point is that they should not be assumed to vitiate religiously based social commitments.

You might say that these are examples of bad therapy. In every case I have described, the therapist was a senior, well-regarded member of the clinical community. And I'd wager that if the therapist had brought up the case in a clinical consultation group, no one would have objected to the interpretations of their clients' community activities. At best, such activities are deemed irrelevant to the business of therapy, and at worst they are deemed indicative of the client's pathology.

When clients bring up their community concerns, the therapist can acknowledge and explore them, but the therapist's initiation of conversation about community service is a much more delicate issue. It is one thing to ask people whether they feel safe in their neighborhood or whether they are being treated fairly by the welfare system. These discussions are part of ecologically sensitive therapy. But it is harder to proactively address the flip side of ecological sensitivity: the client's potential contribution to the community. We therapists tend to stay mired in the language of individual self-interest and our mandate to promote that self-interest. We don't want to impose our beliefs and expectations about how clients should be living their social or political lives. And most clients come to therapy expecting private, personal discussions, not discussions of broader social issues. Over generations, we have shaped what people expect to tell us and hear from us.

This is where we have to believe in the intimate bond between self and community. Feminists have pointed out how healing it can be to victimized women to become involved in public service and activism to help other women facing similar traumas.[22] In this and other equally obvious situations, the therapist can broach the idea, when the time is right clinically, of the client engaging in community service activities. From the moral perspective, how the therapist frames such a recommendation or inquiry is critical: if it is put only in terms of self-interest ("I think this would be good for you") and not also in terms of acting on an internal moral standard of service to others, then an opportunity is lost to promote moral growth as well as psychological healing. The involvement with the community may last only as long as there are immediate benefits to the client.

Ideally, the therapist and the client can create a discourse that does justice to the healing power of moral commitment to help others. Many people who have suffered a great loss or who are recovering from a problem such as alcoholism articulate a sense of obligation or calling to help others facing the same challenges. (In Alcoholics Anonymous, they call it the "twelfth step.") These people know that helping others also helps themselves, but they do not experience self-improvement as their primary motivation. There is a moral quality to their thinking, a sense of obligation they embrace that they did not create on their own. As therapists, we can affirm these moral commitments as the essence of both personal healing and social responsibility.

Not all clients have experienced a loss or trauma that elicits the desire to help others similarly afflicted. With them we can be proactive in a different way. We can ask during the first session, or even on intake forms, about the client's involvement in groups and activities in the community. I would bet that most therapists do not currently inquire about, or know much about, their clients' community activities, unless the client brings it up as part of the clinical problem. What we ask about signals to the client what we think is important. The important information we acquire early in therapy about the client's level of community involvement and attitudes toward the community can then be woven into later therapy discussions.

In the first session of a marital therapy case, Norma said that she had never worked outside the home, that she was "just a housewife." When I inquired about her other activities, she told me of her extensive leadership roles in the volunteer sector of her community. Later, when she began to denigrate her community role in contrast to the overriding importance to her of her troubled marriage, I was able to reaffirm the inherent value of what she had done for others outside the family, while agreeing with her that she and her husband had some important internal work to do. She was then able to curtail her community leadership activities to work on her marriage for the time being without rejecting the altruistic side of herself. In the seasons of a person's life, there are times to focus more on community and times to focus more on family. I am confident that Norma will serve the community in the future even better now that she has salvaged a failing marriage that had been a drag on her emotional energies for years.

In the final phase of therapy, I have begun to ask a new question: "How can you use what you have learned in therapy to contribute in your work or community setting, or how are you already using what you have learned?" I wait until the conclusion of cases in which the clients and I agree that they have made considerable gains in therapy; the question would be presumptuous in unsuccessful therapy, and premature when clients are struggling to make headway in the early stages of therapy. My clients generally have no lack of stories and examples. One engineer said he had already helped make his work team more humane by listening more and not wearing down people who disagreed with him. He was proud that he had improved the work environment for his colleagues and supervisees. A new school counselor said she was much more emotionally available to the children and their parents, and as a result she was becoming influential in the school more quickly than she had imagined. She hoped to use this influence to help create a more child- and family-sensitive school.

Fred, a social services administrator, was eager to address the question of how his therapy helped him contribute to his work setting. It came down to moral courage. He used to flinch and flee from tense interpersonal situations when someone was being mistreated or lied to. Now he was able to take a stand for what he thought was right. He gave an example of a potentially compromising situation: he was given information—and told to keep it secret—that a fellow employee was being lied to and unfairly set up for dismissal. He blew the whistle on the situation and in the process defined himself as a person of integrity who would not stand still for such shenanigans. His courage carried the day, and the experience put him in a stronger leadership position in his work setting.

In my discussion with Fred, I noted how much better he felt about himself when he acted this way at work. But I went on to stress what an important thing he had done for his fellow employee who was about to be exploited, and in turn for other workers in his agency who were vulnerable. A healthier work environment would also mean better service to clients. Fred had not picked up any new moral beliefs during the course of his therapy—he knew what was fair and unfair—but he had gained the *courage* of his moral convictions. Being better able to withstand the heat of intense interpersonal conflict, Fred was now a more effective moral agent in the community.

This is an example of how a dual focus on the interior and exterior world can work synergistically and, in particular, of why good personal and interpersonal work in therapy can provide the client with the ingredients to be more effective in the community, especially in situations of tension or conflict. Psychotherapy can be a moral laboratory that prepares people to approach work and community problems with self-awareness and interpersonal sensitivity coupled with moral awareness and moral courage—powerful vehicles for social influence.

If therapists can learn to integrate a vision of community into our therapy, we may be able to reverse psychotherapy's contribution to the increasing self-orientation of contemporary life. We alone will not be able to check the larger forces breaking down community; psychotherapy is not powerful enough for that. But we can stop contributing to the problem and join with other groups promoting the reintegration of individuals and families in communities of justice and concern.[23]

What does such a vision require of therapists? Just as we cannot help clients with feelings we cannot accept in ourselves, we cannot weave community themes into our therapy unless we are working on our own responsibilities as members of the community. I am certainly not advocating that all therapists quit their clinical practices and feed the homeless full-time or run for political office. But I do think we need to expand our horizon of concern and commitment beyond our office and our friends and family. When we ourselves see the connections between our own private and public lives, we will be able to extend our habits of the heart to the wider society.

When I first started to do therapy with chronically ill people and their families, I thought I could confine my knowledge and expertise to the clinical situation. I didn't need to know much or do much about health insurance, the vagaries of multispecialty medical centers, and the maze of roles in teaching hospitals. I eventually learned that I could not help my clients if I did not become an activist in the larger health care system. I am now as committed to changing that system as I am to helping particular individuals and families.

Community advocacy, however, need not entail vilifying other professionals and institutions. What I have learned with difficulty over years of working in medical settings is that I must apply the same ethical standards of respect and fairness to other professionals and managers in the health care system as I apply to my clients. I may challenge them as I challenge my clients, and I may help mobilize consumer pressure, but I must not intentionally deceive or manipulate these individuals or denigrate them personally for the sake of my clients or my social cause. Vilifying and objectifying those we see as blocking social justice or humane treatment perpetuates the cycle of social injustice and inhumane treatment. And it undermines therapists' moral credibility with our clients, who see us selectively apply standards of fairness and truthfulness to those we agree with and not to those we disagree with.

Chief candidates for villain status among therapists are managed health care organizations and health maintenance organizations, which are requiring therapists to change their accustomed ways of working. Although these organizations are far from perfect in their operations, therapists have to accept some responsibility for the problem. Like medical physicians, psychotherapists until recently have tended to operate in a clinical vacuum without sufficient regard for conserving human and fiscal resources. Now that increases in health care costs have become virtually unbearable for society, therapists are being reined in along with other health professionals. Although therapists must continue to challenge the hegemony of the economic approach to mental health care, we must also be humble about our own past failure to appreciate the broader societal context of our work. In the 1970s and 1980s private practice therapists learned to charge what "the market will bear" and to see length of therapy as a matter of therapeutic style and client preference, without much regard for the costs. In the 1990s the market struck back, and government regulators started paying more attention.

Just like clients, therapists must now deal with broader market and community forces in the treatment room. The resulting partnership potentially could offer good therapy at an affordable cost to individuals, corporations, and society. But many therapists are experiencing terror about their future economic viability, hardly a feeling conducive to good decision making about how much service to offer clients. Therapists, realizing that no one else cares very much about whether they make a lot of money, will have to assert more than their economic interests. They will have to offer a clinical and moral vision for the practice of their healing art in this increasingly resource-limited, market-driven, and often dehumanizing world. Without this vision, psychotherapists will lose their hold on the humane values of the civil society. Their voice will be subsumed by the market and the state, by economics and regulation, by the bottom line and the fine print. The alternative is clear: therapists must participate in, and help shape, a nonpolarizing community dialogue that embraces the legitimate concerns of economists and public officials for the prudent use of resources and protection of the public welfare, while at the same time emphasizing that psychotherapy is a profoundly human form of treatment for troubled people that requires high levels of creativity and spontaneity from the therapist. An overregulated psychotherapy ceases to be therapy; a laissez-faire psychotherapy risks wasting resources and harming clients. A community-sensitive therapy seen as a constructive partnership between the client, the therapist, the government, and the payers of therapy in the community—that is an outcome devoutly to be wished.

We spend our lives in communities that form us and are in turn shaped by us. But we have inherited a tradition of psychotherapeutic discourse that makes this dimension of life nearly invisible and conversation about it nearly inaudible. Over the past fifteen years, therapists have begun to open wide the channel to conversation about how the community affects people who come to therapy. More recently, and more tentatively, therapists have been opening another channel to conversation about how people who come to therapy affect their communities and about how market forces and government regulation are shaping the practice of psychotherapy itself. I believe we are creating the possibility of a different kind of private and public conscience in psychotherapy, one that can help revive the civil society in our communities and nation, if it is not too late.

PART II

THE MORAL CHARACTER OF THE THERAPIST

CHAPTER 6

Caring

THERE IS AN OPEN SECRET AMONG THERAPISTS, ONE WE don't talk about much and certainly don't write about. Despite our intense rivalries and debates about models and techniques of therapy—psychodynamic versus cognitive-behavioral versus family systems versus a hundred other variations—when it comes to referring a family member or close friend to a therapist, we think first of the kind of person the therapist is. Will my sister be in the hands of a good person, a kind, respectful human being as well as a skilled therapist? If a serious crisis occurs during the course of therapy, will this therapist have the wisdom and fortitude to handle it without overreacting or underreacting? Will the therapist care? These questions revolve around the personal qualities that are the focus for this section of the book: caring, courage, and prudence.

These three qualities of character do not, of course, exhaust the range of virtues required to be a good therapist; in fact, earlier chapters highlighted the therapist's virtues of valuing justice and community and being truthful. But I believe that caring, courage, and prudence are especially worthy of full-length treatment. This chapter introduces the idea of virtue and takes up the virtue of caring.

We all know that it takes more than knowledge and skill to be a good therapist. It takes certain qualities of character, or what the Greeks called "virtues." Virtue can be defined as a predisposition to do what is good or right. Having the virtue of honesty, for example, means that you reflexively give others their due—repaying debts, presenting your accomplishments accurately in a job interview—without calculating the benefits and costs of being honest. Virtue, of course, is always defined and practiced within a cultural, religious, or professional tradition; the norms for virtuous behavior change over time. But all cultures have ideas about the qualities of a good person.[1]

Virtue ethics was popular among the humanist Greek philosophers—think of Socrates as a man of wisdom and courage—and among scholastic philosophers such as Thomas Aquinas, who rooted the virtues in theological terms. But virtue ethics fell out of favor after the Middle Ages. When Benjamin Franklin and others resurrected virtues in the eighteenth century, they recast them in the form of desirable qualities of middle-class white males—cleanliness, thrift, and so forth. Virtue ethics subsequently went underground again, resurfacing only in the last fifteen years, when there has been major interest among philosophers and professional ethicists in virtues.[2]

A principal reason ethicists have returned to virtues is the same reason health professionals can profit from looking at virtues: we cannot escape the centrality of the person who is making moral decisions or who is providing health care. Psychotherapy ethics currently is dominated by the rule-oriented approach: respect confidentiality, promote the client's interests rather than our own, practice within our competence, don't have sex with clients, and so forth. These rules establish the outer limits of ethical behavior for therapists but do not touch the character of the therapist and how it affects the clinical relationship and the success of therapy. We need rules, of course, to distill the consensus of the profession about unethical behavior. But we all know therapists who keep all the rules—and practice competent therapy—but lack certain intangible qualities of character. We would never refer a relative or close friend to them.

One problem with virtue ethics has been the tendency to create laundry lists of desirable human qualities—truthfulness, honesty, integrity, fairness, humility, temperance, trustworthiness, loyalty. It can sound like Boy Scouts and Girl Scouts. A way around the laundry list approach is to determine which of the general virtues are relevant in particular contexts and for particular groups, such as therapists. Granted, we all have the obligation to be decent human beings—to be truthful and honest and loyal, for example—but what are the special qualities therapists must have in abundance to do their job well? What are the virtues that therapists must develop to a higher degree than, say, engineers or lawyers?

As the bioethicists Edmund Pellegrino and David Thomasma have noted, a virtue-based professional ethic must be closely linked to the nature of the profession itself.[3] MacIntyre also grounds virtues in the nature of the professional practice. For example, we all have an obligation to respect the earth, but farmers, by the nature of their profession, have a special duty to leave the land in a condition that future generations can cultivate. A highly productive farmer who exhausts the land for the next generation is not a good farmer in the moral sense.[4]

What, then, is the core of psychotherapy from which the central virtues emerge as the sine qua nons of being a good therapist? Writing more generally about health professionals, Pellegrino and Thomasma maintain that "the moral essence of a health profession is the special relationship that sickness and the response to illness creates between healer and patient. . . . The virtues of special interest arise from the caring bond (which includes healing, caring, and curing) and the public trust implied by the commitment for care for another."[5]

A central virtue for therapists, then, as well as for other health professionals, is the ability and predisposition to care for those who entrust their pain to us. Perhaps even more than in other health care settings, the caring bond therapists offer to clients is the heart of the process and the central vehicle for our effectiveness. The empirical evidence for this assertion lies in many decades' worth of research showing that the therapist's ability to create a warm, accepting atmosphere is a principal healing component in all forms of psychotherapy. Its absence is a primary cause of therapeutic failure.[6]

Caring, then, is the cornerstone virtue for therapists. The following illustration from Viktor Frankl, the famous psychotherapist and founder of logotherapy, shows how caring supersedes the techniques we often believe are the curative factor in treatment.

> Recently, I received a telephone call at three in the morning from a lady who told me that she was determined to commit suicide but was curious to know what I would say about it. I replied with all the arguments against this resolution and for survival, and I talked to her for thirty minutes—until she finally gave her word that she would not take her life but rather come to see me in the hospital. But when she visited me there it turned out that not one of all the arguments I offered had impressed her. The only reason she had decided not to commit suicide was the fact that, rather than growing angry because of having been disturbed in my sleep in the middle of the night, I had patiently listened to her and talked with her for half an hour, and a world—she found—in which this can happen, must be a world worth living in.[7]

During the phone call with the client, Frankl was conscious of his therapeutic techniques aimed at convincing her to live at least through the night. He was not conscious of his caring attitude, his immediate responsiveness to the desperation of another human being, even at the cost to his comfort and sleep. Although therapists sometimes take their care for granted, clients do not. They know the real thing when they feel it come their way.

If caring is so central to the practice of psychotherapy, why is the psychotherapy literature so silent on it? There is, of course, a psychotherapy literature on "joining" with clients and establishing an empathetic relationship.[8] But therapists' caring behavior is generally viewed only as a means to an end, a way to establish a therapeutic relationship and thus to treat the client, not as the essential moral prerequisite for psychotherapy. Therapists, like physicians and lawyers, are more comfortable with the language of techniques than with the language of morality, with skills-talk more than virtues-talk.

The psychologist Seymour Sarason claims that the major "helping" professions in the United States (medicine, psychology, teaching, and law) have systematically deemphasized the role of caring and compassion.[9] This deemphasis reflects a larger cultural lionizing of rationality and technology in American life. After all, isn't it better to be hard-nosed than softheaded? Interestingly, Sarason also believes that caring and compassion have become casualties of American individualism, because clients who are stripped of their social context are more likely to be seen as categories—as their disease, their IQ, their legal status.[10]

To this point, a senior family medicine teacher once told me about the temptation for young hospital-based resident physicians to regard frail elderly patients as only "that senile old lady" or that "cantankerous old man." He said that in his private practice he sees patients for many years and knows their histories and their families. He knows that they have children and dote over their grandchildren, that they worked hard and contributed their talents to their community. They are known people with a known social context; they cannot be summed up by their current physical state.

Caring, then, is not just a frill in the helping professions. It is an essential lubricant for the flow of mutual understanding, which is, after all, the heart of a helping relationship. A lawyer who does not care is not likely to understand what a divorcing client really wants. A surgeon who does not care is not likely to understand the patient's ambivalence about undergoing a surgical procedure. Sometimes these professionals can "fill in" their partial understanding if they share the patient's culture or ethnicity, but truly understanding someone from a different social group requires a well-developed ability to listen, learn, and be present.[11]

Caring, of course, means different things to different people. The philosopher Nel Noddings, who is influenced by Martin Buber's relational ethics, places caring in the context of relationship rather than viewing it as an individual attitude or set of behaviors. A caring relationship, according to Noddings, involves three elements on the part of the "one-caring": receptivity to the other, an "engrossment in the other," and a "motivational shift" toward the other and toward the other's ends or goals.[12]

The first two elements, receptivity and engrossment, both involve feeling with the other and sensitivity to the other at particular moments during the relationship. The notion of receptivity is similar to that of empathy, but Noddings prefers the traditionally feminine metaphor of receptivity to the traditionally masculine metaphor of projective empathy. The one-caring is letting the other in, feeling *with* the other rather than just figuring *out* the other. For therapists, the difference is between knowing that someone is depressed and also being able to be with this person emotionally in the experience of sadness and despair.

Engrossment refers to those occasions when the one-caring allows the other to "fill the firmament" in the form of focused attention. For these moments, the one-caring is saying, with his or her attentiveness, "You are the total focus of my concern right now. There is nothing to distract me from attending to you." For clients in psychotherapy, experiencing this engrossed concern and attention from the therapist brings a powerful sense of being important, accepted, affirmed, and even loved. For therapists, allowing ourselves to be engrossed with our clients makes the work at once immensely fulfilling and terribly challenging. The therapist must have a solid sense of self in order to maintain personal and professional boundaries and to keep a dual focus on the client's experience and his or her own internal experience. We must become engrossed in our clients' experience without losing ourselves there. I elaborate later on the challenges to maintaining caring relations in psychotherapy.

The third element in Nodding's theory of caring is a willingness to assist with the other's agenda rather than promoting your own. This may seem obvious: promoting the welfare of the client is the first responsibility of a professional. The rub comes when the client and I define this welfare differently. I may wish that the abused woman would leave her husband, but she may want to stay and try to work out the problem. I have known women who felt deeply cared for by counselors in women's shelters until they announced that they wanted to go back to their husband or boyfriend, whereupon the shelter staff moved into a more coercive and less caring mode of relating. When the client's goals or expectations do not match with our professional or personal agendas, it can be difficult to maintain a caring relation. The following case taught me an important lesson about this issue early in my career.

Florence was a forty-five-year-old single parent with a sixteen-year-old daughter and a thirteen-year-old son. She initiated therapy after her daughter took the SAT exam stoned on marijuana and, naturally, did quite poorly. This was a wake-up call to Florence about her daughter's problems. Florence herself had a serious medical problem: multiple sclerosis diagnosed seven years before. Her MS had taken a downward course from the beginning, with none of the comforting remissions that many others experience. She could still walk with the help of canes, but her life was fairly constricted. She was frustrated and intermittently depressed over her health, and she was worried about her daughter and about whether she could maintain control over her strapping young son. To top things off, she was furious with the medical and social service agencies that were providing her services.

In the therapy, we got to work immediately on the substance abuse and related risky behaviors her daughter was involved in. After initially running away from home, her daughter began to settle down. During these early sessions, we also discussed Florence's health concerns and her children's worries about her, as well as her level of stress and her anger at the agencies. After about seven sessions, I suggested a one-to-one session with Florence to talk about her problems that were unrelated to her children. During this session, she was not herself: she was alternately discouraged and distracted, with little of the fire and can-do attitude that had come through even in the darkest days before.

When I asked Florence what was going on, she told me she didn't like coming to therapy by herself without the children. She was a patient everywhere else in her life—with doctors, home health nurses, the Social Security Administration, and many more. With me, she had felt like a responsible parent trying to do a better job caring for her children. Along the way, she didn't mind talking about her health as it affected her and her children. But she hated being cast as a needy patient.

When I work with single-parent families, my custom is to have several individual sessions with the parent to discuss personal issues, which can be explored more deeply without the children present. Florence's discomfort took me by surprise; generally, single parents enjoy one-to-one time in therapy. But she experienced private sessions as undermining her sense of competence and independence. This was a choice point for me. I could easily have assumed there were only pathological reasons for her resistance to private sessions and then pursued its deeper meaning—thereby telling her I did not agree with her ideas about how she should be helped. I could have viewed her resistance as a tactic to control the therapy, perhaps by hiding behind the children, and then reasserted my judgment that individual sessions were in her best interests. Or I could have cleverly appeared to yield while actually retaining my control—for example, by granting her permission to convene our next private session when she was ready.

Instead, I simply acknowledged what she was saying, explored for a while what she meant, accepted her wishes, and thanked her for her honesty and forthrightness in speaking up for what she wanted and needed. It was okay with me that she wanted me as her family therapist, not her individual therapist. She needed most of all to be in the driver's seat in her life, a metaphor made poignant by her increasing difficulty handling her automobile. I did not experience my agreement primarily as a therapeutic strategy, but as a decision that was clear once I let in her pain and her wishes. Although my stance may have been an effective strategy (a power struggle would have been counterproductive), I think Florence experienced it fundamentally as a caring response to her. She taught me something important about setting aside my accustomed therapeutic techniques when they get in the way of being able to see past categories ("single parent," "MS patient") and recognize a client as a unique person with a unique agenda.

The treatment went on to a successful conclusion for all three family members. Florence wrote me years later to say that her children were becoming successful adults, that she was doing well emotionally, but that unfortunately her disease had continued its destructive course unabated.

Caring for Florence and her children was not difficult for me. My response, in Noddings's terms, was one of "natural caring," which stems from a spontaneous desire to receive and respond to the other.[13] The paradigmatic example is the caring of a parent for a child. Natural caring comes most easily when the client is similar to the therapist in some way, shows pain directly, asks for help, and responds appreciatively when the therapist offers it. Natural caring is not automatic even in these ideal situations, however, because professional and personal barriers can interfere. But the lubricant for care is in place in the positive feelings and the sense of identification that the client elicits in the therapist.

Not so for the "difficult" client who is unlike the therapist in important ways, hides pain, is ambivalent about receiving help, or complains that the therapist is not solving his or her problems. Whereas natural caring involves the ability to respond spontaneously to those who entrust their pain to us, "ethical caring" takes over when spontaneous sentiments are not available to help make a caring connection. In these situations, according to Noddings, we call upon our ethical ideal of being "one-who-cares" in order to feel sensitivity and responsivity to someone for whom our natural inclinations are not sufficient. In fact, we may dislike the person and feel appalled at his or her conduct. Ethical caring derives from the sense that we *must* try to respond to the other. Noddings believes that the ethical ideal we call upon in these situations emerges from our own experiences of being cared for as children and throughout our lives. These experiences and memories give us the strength "to strive to meet the other morally."[14] It is like having residual sources of water when the regular well is not yielding its usual amount, water that was mostly given us by other important people in our lives.

We have all encountered clients who turn us off personally. The biggest turnoff for most therapists, I believe, is the client who denies personal responsibility for problems, who expects the therapist to fix things, and who is never satisfied with the therapist's performance. Most of us know that we cannot help someone we don't care for, and that we cannot care unless we find something in the person's pain or joy to respond to. The actual work of ethical caring comes in the search for a way to let our insides connect with the insides of the client. I think of it as trying to find a handle, an anchor point, to use in moving myself into a position of caring and compassion. Sometimes my colleagues help me see the client in a different light, and sometimes I find my way there on my own with the help of the client, as the next case illustrates.

Brad called to seek help for his troubled marriage to Nancy. Both were in their midforties, and it was a second marriage for each of them; all the children were gone from home. For openers, Nancy said she was furious with Brad for not consulting her on decisions about money and for his patronizing attitude toward her. Brad expressed frustration with Nancy for browbeating him about his lifestyle (too busy and sports-oriented). An accountant, he was a novice to feelings-talk but wanted to save his marriage. His willingness to learn, despite a tendency to monologue, gave me an opening to like him and spontaneously care for him. Nancy, a businesswoman with a fair amount of prior therapy experience, was much harder for me to like.

My difficulty with Nancy began with breathtaking quickness, when she complained angrily at the outset of the first session that I had not told them the suite number of my office, causing them to waste time searching the building. Later in the session, she complained about the temperature in the therapy room, for which I apologized, saying that the maintenance people were trying to adjust the thermostat. She suggested that they might not pay for the session if they couldn't even be physically comfortable. In between these criticisms of the environment of therapy, Nancy raged at her husband and mocked his analytical style when he spoke ponderously. She revealed little personal pain beneath her anger. Brad, for his part, was doing his best to create a triangle with me by looking at me and rolling his eyes during her outbursts.

I got through the first session in a reasonably nonreactive and supportive manner, but inside I was frightened by Nancy. I have had the experience of feeling intimidated by clients whom I also liked in some ways, for example, clients who show both rage and hurt, allowing me to connect enough with their hurt to sustain me when their anger turns against me. But with Nancy in the first session I could find no positive feeling within me to hold on to. My natural caring had taken the day off.

In these situations, I take stock of my own reactions and make the establishment of a caring connection to the client my top priority, because without it I will not be able to be a good therapist for that person. My first step with Nancy was to reflect, after the difficult first session, about the source of her fury. I realized that I did not yet have a clear picture of her complaints about her marriage, and of Brad's contributions to the problems, because I got lost in her delivery of her complaints—many of which came in generalizations and personality attacks. I considered the possibility that Nancy had a borderline personality disorder, but I was reluctant to draw that conclusion so soon. And perhaps her anger at me stemmed from a sense of shame, a kind of anticipatory shot to alert me to what a terrible person she felt she was.

These were my reflections at the cognitive level. At the emotional level, my fear began to be joined with a sense of challenge. Now at least I knew what to expect. As I prepared for the second session, I knew that I had to set limits on Nancy's destructive verbal behavior in the session in order to do good therapy and to position myself to be able to care for her. I knew I couldn't learn to care for her unless I could create a more respectful atmosphere in the room.

In the second session, I gently but firmly confronted Nancy about her interrupting behavior and then about her mocking behavior. Her response was one of grudging respect that I had called her on these behaviors, which she said she knew were not constructive. She stopped mocking and interrupting, but when her turn came to speak, she still continued the verbal barrage against her husband. Despite my efforts to get beneath the surface, she showed no other feelings. (I was also working with Brad on his issues, and on couples issues, but for the purposes of this illustration I am focusing on my relationship with Nancy.)

The breakthrough came in the third session, when I spent part of the time talking to Nancy and Brad separately. I have learned, when working with couples, that if I cannot find a way to like and care for one of the partners, it helps to meet separately, to establish a one-to-one link. I talked with Nancy alone first, then with Brad. Outside of the angry force field between her and Brad, I told Nancy that I felt there was something I was not understanding in the intensity of her anger, and I wondered if she felt I was not "getting it." She readily agreed and then talked with despair about how she felt she was losing her control of her life in this relationship, how she had been functioning well since ending her former marriage but was feeling increasingly incompetent and out of control since she remarried. She filled in details about their marital interactions that made her feelings fully understandable to me for the first time. Although she seemed to control the couple's verbal interactions and was clearly in charge of her business, she felt controlled by Brad on most decisions in her family life. Nancy felt like a child. Her anger came from hopelessness. I said, "You must feel like you are drowning," and she responded, "Exactly." We connected.

From that moment on, I was able to care for Nancy with my natural sentiment of caring. I could see both her wounds and her anger. I could advocate for her to regain control of her life, while at the same time I could advocate for Brad to be treated respectfully by Nancy when she was angry at him. I could handle with equanimity Nancy's occasional flare-ups at me. I could both empower her and challenge her because I had found a way to care.

Every therapist has stories like this one, when our natural caring does not get us very far and we must call upon ethical reserves to help us hang in there until we can respond to the client. I visualize this process as one of continually repositioning myself with the client until something gets through to me. For some, I might listen in a different way—like tuning to a different radio frequency—that allows me to respond with compassion. For others like Nancy, I might have to first challenge negative behavior and then move into a receptive mode. For someone who has sexually abused others, it might mean shifting the conversation for a time to the person's own experience of being abused. For one man who seemed unreachable and disconnected from his feelings, the moment came when I encouraged him to tell me at length about a difficult and successful building project he had conducted for his company. I sensed his pride in his achievement, and I was able to relish the experience with him. In these situations, ethical caring keeps me afloat like a life preserver until my natural buoyancy reemerges.

The barriers to the virtue of caring come in several forms. For starters, there are clients for whom ethical caring never leads to natural caring. A child psychologist realized that she was struggling without success to be emotionally responsive to a child's parents. When they asked for more help from her, she referred them to a family therapist. Some therapists do not work with sexual abusers because they realize that they cannot be sensitive and caring enough with these individuals. I think therapists should find a way to avoid taking on clients whom they will have grave difficulty caring for, as long as there are other therapists who are likely to be better positioned emotionally to deal with them.

The situation is more difficult when the therapist expects to find a way to care for a client but eventually finds it impossible. Sometimes the therapist must continue to do his or her best because another therapist is no more likely to have any success in caring for the client. But often the therapy languishes, and the client senses the therapist's difficulty in emotionally investing. The therapist can then initiate a discussion about whether the therapy is helpful to the client and about other options for treatment. The challenge is to have this discussion in a nonrejecting way, in the spirit of ethical caring.

In my own experience with barriers to caring, I tend to stubbornly hold on, trying to find an opening for caring. I have never had a client for more than a few sessions for whom I did not find at least some small way to care. Sometimes, however, I am not fully conscious of how hard it has been for me until the therapy ends, at which point I am massively relieved. And when such a client has called back months or years later requesting further help, I have been immediately repulsed by the idea of seeing that person again. I realize that ethically I should not take back someone I dread seeing because I once had so much difficulty caring. What I do in these (fortunately infrequent) circumstances is suggest that a new therapist might be better. If they are willing (all have been so far), I help them find the right therapist and, with their permission, share my experience with the new therapist. All clients deserve a therapist who can give them both ethical and natural caring.

In addition to the barriers that clients bring to the caring relationship and the ones therapists bring, both idiosyncratic and developmental, there are barriers built into the medical model of diagnosis and treatment that most therapists learn and practice. We learn to use labels that, if we are not careful, can objectify our clients. I am not antilabel or antidiagnosis; it is useful to know if the client is clinically depressed or schizophrenic, or if the relationship is abusive. The danger comes from the tendency of the clinical label to become so figural that the client's personal context becomes invisible. We end up describing and relating to the person as a problem, a deficit, a category, instead of as a complex human being with a problem. We do precisely what we criticize medical physicians for doing, namely, relating to the patient as a diagnosis or a label, not as a person.

This noncaring stance is seen most readily in therapists' verbal discourse about clients, both in casual conversations and in more formal case consultations. "Wendy is a borderline" is an apparently neutral statement that carries with it the danger of objectifying Wendy as a personality disorder, especially if what follows describes only her deficits. Furthermore, a negative emotional tone is audible when the therapist says things such as, "Wendy is a typical borderline; you know how they are," or, "Jim is a full-blown narcissist." Often these are not neutral clinical descriptions; the nonverbals that accompany such statements often bespeak a struggle within the therapist to care for a challenging client. We think we are describing the client when actually we are saying more about our own feelings. When we have a problem caring for a client, we make it the client's problem instead of our own. I believe this is one of the fundamental ethical challenges for therapists, and one of our most common serious ethical lapses. Yet the objectifying of clients therapists dislike does not appear as an issue in any professional ethics codes that I am aware of.

Now there is nothing wrong with having angry feelings toward our clients. Likewise, there is a difference between ventilating negative affect about clients, which can help therapists go back and care, and the kind of objectifying that diminishes the capacity to care for them. An example of ventilating is my recounting, in a case consultation with colleagues, of how I felt like leaping at the throat of a man who was incredibly nasty and patronizing to his wife in the first therapy session and who smirked at me when I challenged him about it. The ensuing discussion helped me clarify that the wife did not seem as bothered as I was, that I felt intimidated by him, and that there was a lot more to learn about where both of them were coming from. We did not give the man a personality label based on limited data, we did not assign him malevolent motives, and we did not pathologize her acceptance of his putdowns. Thus, even though I was showing a lot of strong negative feelings about the client, the consultation process ultimately facilitated caring and professional responsibility. Importantly, the consultation experience for me was one of being cared for, enabling me to avoid rejecting my client.

Contrast that scenario with a more negative one: five minutes before a session with a client, I shared the following conversation with a colleague in the staff lounge, with two other therapists standing around:

COLLEAGUE (*wearily*): Would anyone like to trade clients for the next hour?

ME: I will. You can have my next one any time you like.

COLLEAGUE: Mine is a ten-year-old.

ME: Mine is developmentally around eight, so you would owe me on this one. And mine is a therapist.

We all had a good chuckle and went about greeting our clients. But I felt badly about my sarcastic putdown of my client. (My colleague had not put down her client but rather seemed only to be expressing fatigue just prior to starting a potentially difficult session.) I realized that I had become impatient and annoyed with my client's whiny complaints, and that I expected more of him because he was also a therapist. Even though my client had not overheard the conversation, I had jeopardized my relationship with him by objectifying him, by using him to appear witty and sophisticated to my colleagues, and by pretending that my comments were all about him and not mainly about me. I had made it more difficult to be in a caring relation with him, not because I was angry or frustrated and had shared those feelings with a colleague, but because I had put down my client without disclosing my own feelings: my sarcastic comment was only about *his* developmental lag, not about *my* frustration. It was a moral lapse on my part, every bit as real as a breach of confidentiality and perhaps more detrimental to the therapy.

After realizing what I had done, and what I was feeling, I recovered my ability to care throughout the rest of the therapy.

Clinical techniques are the great double-edged sword of psychotherapy. They are the vehicle for delivering therapy, but they can also be a haven for a heartless therapist. Every therapist has a responsibility to develop and refine a range of therapeutic behaviors associated with his or her model of therapy. The danger occurs when we use a technique without sensitive regard for the needs and goals of the client. In an instructive study of first- and second-year family therapy trainees, Stolk and Perlesz found that second-year trainees had learned more skills since their first year

but were more alienating to clients. Clients found them less compassionate and caring.[15] Eve Lipchik, a skilled practitioner of
brief, solution-focused therapy, has written about therapists new
to the model who sometimes use the techniques before having
connected with the client and against the sometimes active resistance of the client.[16] In these cases, when the caring relation never
takes hold, the techniques become oppressive. And the therapists
become morally weaker.

I knew a therapist who, when challenged about whether his
approach to therapy was sufficiently caring, would reply that, of
course, you have to show clients warmth and caring at the beginning in order to "pull their strings" later in the therapy. This difference between "showing" care and "being" caring illustrates
well the difference between the virtue of caring and the technique
of showing caring behaviors. The irony is that I knew this therapist to be caring with clients, but he was caught in a discourse for
explaining his work that disdained the mushy language of care
and sensitivity. It becomes a serious problem when these senior
therapists—who developed the virtue of caring early in their
careers and now take it for granted—get involved in training
young therapists who buy the technological approach to therapy
without a grounding in the relational foundations. Therapy train-
ers have a responsibility to the next generation to not be silent
about the centrality of caring in the practice of their profession.

I don't subscribe to the idea that some clinical techniques are
inherently caring and others are not. It is possible to use interpretations of unconscious material in an uncaring way, and to use
paradoxical techniques in a caring way. (Paradoxical techniques
are strategies such as urging the client to continue to enact a symp-
tom, such as asking someone who worries too much to schedule
time each day to worry, thereby deliberately controlling something
that seemed uncontrollable.) The key is the therapist's attitude and
intent, which are often revealed best in postsession conversations
among colleagues. If the therapist conveys a sense of having

"nailed" the client with an insight, or having "faked out" the client with a paradox, then chances are the technique was used in an objectifying, noncaring manner. At their worst, therapists can sound no different from the overworked and frustrated medical residents I have overheard relishing the opportunity to do an uncomfortable procedure on a "hateful" patient. These feelings are human and should not be suppressed; I do not advocate a therapist thought-police patrolling case consultations. Rather, these feelings are something to be worked through, not projected onto our clients.

The final barriers I want to mention are contextual: the settings we work in and the cultures we live in. According to Noddings's theory, the one-caring must receive support by being cared for and treated fairly; otherwise, sustained caring is impossible for most people.[17] Unsupportive and alienating work settings inevitably affect therapists' ability to care, especially for difficult clients at the end of a long workday or workweek. Having our work undermined by other professionals in positions of greater institutional power erodes motivation and investment in clinical care. Seeing too many clients during a workweek does the same, as does having to fit the client's needs to the rigidly enforced restrictions of managed care contracts. Therapists start to go through the motions, it shows, and we know it. We become negative about our clients, we hope for no-shows and cancellations, our natural caring declines, and our ethical caring begins to feel like martyrdom. When such conditions arise, it is time to change the context or get out, in my view, because we cannot sustain the fundamental virtue of caring.

Barriers to care show themselves particularly with clients from cultures or social class groups different from our own or from groups whose members are not represented well on the clinical staff. If caring is based on developing understanding, it is tested every time we work with people with whom we do not share a life world. This is particularly true when clients believe they have reason to distrust us, based on their past experience with professionals. The result can be wariness and objectification on both sides. The clients do not continue in therapy, and the therapists fault the clients without examining whether the culture of therapy is offering an experience of understanding and care to all its potential clients.[18]

There are dangers in focusing on the virtue of caring in psychotherapy. The first is the risk that being emotionally receptive and responsive will cause the therapist to lose his or her boundaries in the clinical relationship. This can take a number of forms, including overidentifying with the client's feelings and needs, being more motivated for change than the client is, carrying the client's burdens home on a regular basis, losing one's good judgment, and becoming personally or sexually involved with the client.[19]

The second important danger of focusing on caring as a virtue is the risk of paternalism. I might overemphasize the curative power of my care, assuming that it magically transforms those who are open to it. Once I define myself as a virtuous, caring therapist, I might come to define everything I do as flowing inexorably from that moral goodness within. I might not work as hard to confirm that my behavior is experienced by the client as caring, I might underestimate the importance of diagnostic understanding and clinical techniques, and I might underestimate the continued discipline required to care in the moral sense.

The third danger stems from a confusion about caring and confronting, the notion that caring always means being supportive and accepting. Noddings refers to the "toughness of caring."[20] Truly taking on the goals of the client means that sometimes I must be forceful and even provocative. The only way I could both help and care for Nancy was to challenge her firmly. This made the relationship safe enough for her to be vulnerable and tempered my own fear, which was blocking my ability to care.

The final danger lies in the potential to split the nurturing and the technical aspects of therapy, the expressive and the instrumental, the intuitive and the rational. As Noddings points out, all caring by professionals involves moving back and forth between a rational problem-solving mode and a receptive-intuitive model.[21] Within their mandate to help their clients, therapists must choose the appropriate mode for the moment. If we focus too much on the expressive mode, we risk becoming lost in the client's emotional force field. If we focus too exclusively on the instrumental mode, we risk becoming unfeeling and unseeing. Caring involves doing whatever is necessary to be helpful, not just feeling with the client.

It is not enough for therapists to believe they are caring; clients must feel it. But how do clients sense that we genuinely care for them? It can be difficult to tell when we are in our therapist mode of active listening and empathic responding. It's our job to act caring, just as it's a lawyer's job to act logical and an engineer's to act practical. I think clients sniff out our genuine feelings for them by our "offstage" behavior: our conversations on the phone at intake and when rescheduling appointments, our banter in the hallway on the way to the therapy room, our spontaneous concern for a client's physical illness or discomfort, and our interest in the welfare of the client's loved ones.

Some years ago, when I supervised family practice residents in an outpatient psychiatry clinic, a psychiatric nurse colleague said that she could always tell without looking up whether a patient was being accompanied down the hall by a family practice resident or by a psychiatry resident. The family practice residents chatted informally with the patients, while the psychiatry residents walked ahead of the patients in silence. Guess who seemed more caring? The small things show nonscripted care, such as offering to get an extra couch pillow for a client with a sore back, or doing our best, within our own limits, to accommodate a schedule change brought about by a client's new job.

Some therapists give large doses of care to their clients while showing indifference for the client's loved ones. When a former client of mine told her previous therapist that her adult son was suddenly acting strangely and threateningly, the therapist recommended calling the police and having them take her son to the county emergency psychiatry clinic. When the client protested that her son would get caught up in the medical-legal system, the therapist told her that it was not her problem. My problem is not with the advice but with the chilling lack of compassion. Truly caring for someone means caring about those they love and have some responsibility for. This therapist was well regarded in the community, but I think she was demonstrating how the therapeutic ethic of individualistic self-interest can block understanding and caring for a client who feels moral responsibility for a loved one's welfare. I believe that the privatized, self-oriented moral stance of much psychotherapy tends ultimately to undermine therapists' ability to care because, as Sarason maintains, sensitivity to social context is essential to understanding and compassion in professional relationships.[22]

This brings us back to the notion of virtue as a predisposition to do what is good or right. The morally caring therapist is prepared to automatically treat the client with sensitivity and respect, whether onstage in the therapy session or offstage in the waiting room or on the telephone, whether looking at baby pictures or fielding complaints about the clinic's billing system, whether talking *with* the client as part of therapeutic discourse or talking *about* the client with colleagues. No one practices the virtue of caring at all times and with all clients, but the caring therapist experiences lapses of caring as unfortunate and tries to learn from them and repair any damage that has occurred.

Therapists, of course, cannot help everyone achieve their goals.

Some problems do not get better, and sometimes progress in one area is snuffed out by deterioration in another. If therapists cannot always promise change, let alone miracles, we can promise to walk with people who entrust themselves to us, to support and challenge them, and to never objectify them or exploit them for our own purposes. In so doing, we enact the quintessential virtue and the primary moral mandate of our profession.

CHAPTER 7

Courage

C OURAGE HAS GOTTEN POOR PRESS IN RECENT YEARS. IT has been ascribed to military officers who lie to Congress to protect illegal covert operations, and to athletes willing to risk sudden cardiac death in order to make millions of dollars. Back in Homer's time perhaps too much was made of courage, and characterizations of it were confined pretty much to men. Courage historically meant someone died, preferably the enemy, but often oneself. Despite this checkered legacy from both the distant and recent past, I want to reclaim the virtue of courage because, simply put, it takes courage to be a good therapist. The best therapists invariably have a goodly supply of it.

Courage may be the least discussed aspect of the character of the therapist. Everyone believes that therapists must be caring individuals, and it makes good sense for a therapist to have practical wisdom, along with truthfulness and commitment to the broader social welfare. But courage, bravery, fortitude? I invite therapist readers of this book to think about your finest hours with your most difficult cases. Ask yourself if these were not moments when you screwed up your courage and did something scary or difficult to help your client, moments when you stretched way past your comfort zone, sessions after which you had to grab a colleague to talk about what just happened.

Courage is a virtue practiced in the present moment but only thought about consciously after the brave deed is completed. While rising to a challenge, people rarely say to themselves, "I am being quite brave here." Often they never think in terms of courage or bravery at all until someone praises them in these terms. In media interviews, people who have done something heroic, such as risking their lives to save a stranger, invariably resist being labeled courageous or heroic, asserting, "I just did what I had to do," or, "I didn't have a choice. The child was going to drown." Partly this reaction stems from modesty, but it also derives, I believe, from the subjective experience of courage itself: it demands absorption in the challenging situation, with a minimum of self-consciousness about the extraordinary nature of one's acts.

Similarly, I began to think about the case illustrations in this chapter in terms of courage, or lack of it, only after applying a retrospective lens; at the time I just remember feeling scared or confused and handling the situation as best I could. But what was operating, I have come to believe, was the virtue of courage, which the *Merriam-Webster Dictionary* defines as "the firmness of spirit that faces danger or extreme difficulty without flinching or retreating." In one of the cases I describe, however, what was operating was a lack of courage.

Lorraine, age forty-five, called to get help managing her life with her husband, James, age fifty, who had Parkinson's disease and Crohn's disease, a serious bowel disorder. They had two teenage girls at home. During the first session with Lorraine and James, I became aware of her extremely close and often-conflicted relationship with her husband's neurologist. Dr. Murphy, who was about her age, was extraordinarily available to Lorraine when she had concerns about her husband's medical problems. I learned from talking with Dr. Murphy that he was acutely aware of the stress on the family since, as he frequently discussed with Lorraine, he himself had an ill spouse. He identified with Lorraine and was open with her, for which she was extremely grateful. Over the years, however, the relationship between Dr. Murphy and Lorraine seesawed: they would be very close and collaborative, but then he would experience her as too demanding of his time and attention and would relate his frustration to the other two physicians on the case, a family physician and a gastroenterologist.

Sometimes Dr. Murphy communicated his frustration directly by telling Lorraine that she was overinvolved and too controlling of her husband, but he still allowed her to do most of the medical negotiations for her husband, who didn't like doctors and was frequently incommunicative. Other times Dr. Murphy withdrew emotionally by being cool and businesslike. Either way, Lorraine responded with anger and hurt; most of all, she was confused about what was going on. She would call or meet with Dr. Murphy without her husband present, and they would have what seemed like a lovers' spat and then make up—for a while.

I entered the picture years into this intense and medically crucial relationship. Lorraine was becoming increasingly frantic about restoring a good relationship with Dr. Murphy. When I gingerly suggested that it sounded like they were having a "lovers' quarrel," Lorraine agreed immediately and James shrugged his shoulders. He didn't much care for Dr. Murphy but had learned as his functioning declined to let his wife handle medical matters. I had hoped to achieve some movement by pointing out how overly intense this clinical relationship was— "lovers' quarrel" is a fairly provocative metaphor—but James didn't much care, and Lorraine just wanted the relationship to get back to the way it had been. Dr. Murphy had become her substitute mate. I was more interested in empowering James to manage his health care and in helping James and Lorraine restore a functioning marriage. But I knew that we had to deal first with the triangle with Dr. Murphy.

As is my custom as a medical family therapist, I arranged a meeting with the couple and Dr. Murphy, having first talked with Dr. Murphy on the phone and heard his complaints about Lorraine and his invitation to me to help him get her to be less demanding of his time and attention and less obsessed with her husband's health. James didn't show up at the meeting in Dr. Murphy's office, and we proceeded without him. Within minutes, I felt as if I were in a marital therapy session, with Lorraine and Dr. Murphy the feuding couple and James their teenage son. Dr. Murphy lectured Lorraine about her unrealistic expectations for her husband's functioning and the kinds of treatments physicians could offer. Lorraine responded with anger, justifying her frequent requests for help from Dr. Murphy and the other physicians involved and telling him that he was having problems handling a family member who wanted to be a full partner in her husband's care. I tried to inject the remark that James was a capable adult who could relate to Dr. Murphy directly, but I got nowhere. The meeting ended in disarray. In retrospect, I regretted proceeding with the meeting in James's absence, but I had felt obligated to use the time we had all set aside.

What I learned in this conference increased my already grave concerns about the potential fallout from this physician-spouse relationship. And I was becoming concerned that James's medical care could be compromised by this power struggle: Dr. Murphy seemed unprofessionally vehement about there being no need for the change in medications that Lorraine was pushing for. And he seemed uninterested in James's other medical problems and how they might interact with the Parkinson's regimen. Dr. Murphy seemed like a decent person, but he was involved way over his head in this case and lacked any source of consultation about how to manage the complex relationship with Lorraine. (He was asking me to change her, not to help him manage his part better.) Therapists have colleagues to turn to for help in sorting out the intricacies of clinical relationships;

physicians generally have nowhere to turn for this kind of perspective.

The tension increased, Lorraine became ill herself with stress-related problems, the children acted out, and Lorraine and James were not getting along well. I gradually helped Lorraine and James see that there was a problem in how each of them was relating to Dr. Murphy. Lorraine decided to ask Dr. Murphy to call a conference for all the health care professionals working with her and James in order to sort out roles and responsibilities. I asked to meet with Dr. Murphy to talk about goals and process for the conference. (I had permission from Lorraine and James for all my contacts with Dr. Murphy.)

At this private meeting, Dr. Murphy looked distressed. He was having serious problems with his ill wife, he said, and he was upset about his relationship with Lorraine and very critical of her as a wife and mother. His animosity toward her was clear—and somewhat chilling. I asked him what I could do to help him. He softened a bit and replied that he wished I could help him figure out what to do with his relationship with Lorraine. That was the moment when I initiated a series of risks that taxed my "firmness of spirit."

I told Dr. Murphy that I heard his discouragement, and I asked him if he would like my help in ending his professional relationship with Lorraine. He said he would like to end it but didn't see how he could since he was James's physician and he did not want to hurt Lorraine. He also didn't want to repeat the old pattern of having a big fight with her, followed by a lulling period of good feelings. He knew he could not be a good doctor to James over the future years of worsening Parkinson's symptoms without regular contact with Lorraine, James's main caregiver. But how could he just "fire" her and her husband? He seemed trapped, angry, bitter, and resigned—not the sort of feelings patients like their doctors to have about them.

I asked, "Would you like me to help you find a way out of your professional relationship with Lorraine and James?" He replied, "Yes, I would." Then I asked, "Do I have your permission to share with Lorraine and James any parts of this conversation that I think might help with a constructive end to the relationship?" He replied affirmatively. I obtained this permission to give myself maximum flexibility and to avoid having to hold the secret of his wishes.

I met with Lorraine and James the next day to talk about the agenda for the case conference. I did not enter the session with a specific plan for how I would handle the information I had gleaned from my meeting with Dr. Murphy; I wanted first to see where Lorraine and James were. Lorraine had high expectations for the case conference; she thought that the meeting would help the three physicians do a better job of coordinating James's care and that she and Dr. Murphy could patch things up again. James, for his part, was pretty skeptical and increasingly troubled about the stress his wife's relationship with Dr. Murphy was causing her.

I then decided that I could not let Lorraine and James walk into the conference not knowing that Dr. Murphy desperately wanted out of his professional relationship with them, that he was not likely to be open with his wishes, and that there was therefore little chance of any constructive outcome from this crucial meeting that had taken months to set up.

So I said just that. Lorraine asked me if I was sharing just an impression that Dr. Murphy wanted to end the relationship with her. I replied that I was quite certain of his wishes and that I had obtained his permission to share our conversation with them at my discretion. I said I was using my discretion now because, given how important this meeting was to her and James and their family, I could not in fairness be silent about what I knew of Dr. Murphy's position. Lorraine was shocked and furious at Dr. Murphy, and for the first time James was upset too. He said, "Well, if he feels that way, we don't want him either."

As they left the session, a stunned Lorraine asked me what she should do next. Should she confront Dr. Murphy with her anger? Should she just back off? Should they call off the family case conference? I urged her and James to talk together about these options and offered to meet before our next regularly scheduled session if they wanted.

I was glad this was my last session of the day, because I was shaken myself. I had never before been the carrier of news that someone wanted to end a relationship with one of my clients. I had never been in the middle between another professional and a client. I had made an exception to the guidelines I teach my students about staying out of triangles and not doing people's work for them. I knew I was on ethically safe ground because I had obtained permission from Dr. Murphy to talk with Lorraine and James. But I was out on a limb clinically. As I reviewed my decision, I realized I had concluded that Dr. Murphy was not going to be straight with Lorraine and James about what he wanted, even in a discussion I might facilitate, and that as a result of his resentment and ambivalence, he could unintentionally play a quite negative role at the case conference and in the future. Here was my situation: I had information from another professional that I believed my clients needed to know to protect themselves from him. I felt no choice but to reveal what I knew.

That night I had to fly out of state to do a workshop the following day. I kept obsessing over my decision and over Lorraine's and James's reactions and pondered my next steps. I felt very vulnerable, as if I had lit a fuse whose path I could not foresee. So I called a trusted out-of-state colleague from the airport and got consultation and feedback. After I described the situation to him, my colleague, who is both a medical physician and a therapist, affirmed that I had done the right thing for my clients. Furthermore, he expressed grave concern for Dr. Murphy, who, he said, was in danger of self-destructing with this case. My colleague reassured me that I had taken a highly unusual but fully appropriate step in an extraordinary situation. He also concurred with my plan for the next step.

Fifteen minutes before my workshop, I was on the phone long-distance to Dr. Murphy, whom I thought I could catch before he started seeing patients in the morning. Fortunately, I got through. I related to him what I had told Lorraine and James. I reported that she was very angry, and I prepared him for two possibilities: he might never see her again, or she might call or show up to express her outrage directly. James, I thought, would just withdraw. He said he was willing to continue as James's doctor and to work with Lorraine, if that would be helpful. I told him that I thought things would work out for the best if he held to his intention to pass James's care on to a colleague. He sounded nervous but relieved that the logjam was beginning to break up.

When I returned from my workshop, I received a phone call from Lorraine, who told me how angry she was with me for being so unprofessional. I replied that we needed to meet to talk about it. At the session, Lorraine was beside herself with anger, and James was puzzled. My prior feeling of vulnerability was back now that I was facing a client furious about something I had done that was outside my normal behavior as a therapist. I was afraid that I would lose Lorraine and James as clients and that my actions would come back to haunt me in the community. The story as recounted by someone else could certainly make me look bad.

Lorraine began by telling me that she had talked to Dr. Murphy, who had assured her that he was not "firing" her and her husband and that he would be happy to continue as James's doctor. This had been one of my worst fears: that Dr. Murphy would not back me up. Lorraine was most incensed about my taking it upon myself to be a go-between. She felt I had protected Dr. Murphy at her expense by being his messenger. And now she wasn't even sure whether I had carried the correct message. She didn't know if she could trust me any longer. What's more, she had discussed the matter with her previous therapist, who agreed with her that I had acted strangely.

When my worst fears are laid out before me this starkly, like many people I often find myself becoming calm and resolute. I told Lorraine and James that they deserved a full explanation of what I had done and that they could decide after our discussion whether they could trust me in the future. I said I completely understood why they were concerned about my actions, because what I did was outside of the normal way I operate. After all, I had been working with them on boundary issues, and here I was apparently violating a boundary. But the bottom line, I told them, was that I could not ethically carry the secret of Dr. Murphy's attitude and intentions because I was convinced that an already unhealthy clinical relationship was going to become more destructive to all of them—and that furthermore, and crucially, Dr. Murphy did not have the wherewithal at this point to level with them. The way he vacillated today, I pointed out, was what he was likely to continue to do, because he felt trapped. When he gave me permission to share my conversation with him, I believed he was inviting me to help him do what he did not feel capable of doing face to face with Lorraine. And with the case conference just days away, I felt an urgency to take action now.

I was declaring myself, my perceptions, and my values and trying to do so in a sensitive way for all concerned. The rest was out of my hands. I was so glad that I had consulted with a trusted and experienced colleague, whose voice was with me during this painful session. "You may get fired by the clients for this," he had said, "but you did the right thing."

The result was positive in both the short run and the long run. Lorraine and James accepted my explanation and regained confidence in me. They found another physician who worked with James as the primary patient and with Lorraine as an appropriately involved spouse. Lorraine took time to grieve the loss of her intense relationship with Dr. Murphy but emerged more eager to improve her relationship with her husband. James became more of a partner to Lorraine, despite his health limitations, and more in charge of his own health care. It was not a smooth path, and they still have a number of problems, but they were freed from an extremely unhealthy triangle with a professional.

I do not want to generalize from the particulars of this case. I recognize that other therapists might have handled the situation differently and perhaps better; a good outcome, after all, does not mean that I did good therapy. And I feel somewhat sheepish about characterizing myself as courageous here; that was not the feeling I experienced at the time. Nonetheless, in retrospect, I do believe that this case called upon my deepest reserves of self-confidence and determination and on my willingness to take emotional and professional risks for the welfare of my clients. It was an opportunity to practice the virtue of courage.

David Waters and Edith Lawrence are among the very few therapists who have written about courage. In their insightful book *Competence, Courage, and Change*, Waters and Lawrence devote a chapter to the issue of courage in clients and in therapists.[1] Courage, they believe, is what gets clients past blocks to their development and what empowers therapists to persevere in difficult clinical situations. Therapists experience the courage to keep caring, the courage to keep trying, and the courage to take clear stands. On the flip side, failures of courage, according to Waters and Lawrence, are most often evinced when therapists allow clients to stay with old patterns instead of moving the therapy to a new level of intensity that might be challenging for the therapist—for example, failing to work vigorously to get a husband into marital therapy and settling for (more comfortable) individual therapy with the wife. Old marital patterns are less likely to change, but the client doesn't know we chose the easy way out and we "have no blood on our hands" because we can disclaim responsibility for the outcome—it was the husband who chose not to participate.[2]

As therapists, according to Waters and Lawrence, "we are taught caution and circumspection, but not courage."[3] Although caution and circumspection are important (as I argue in the next chapter on prudence), without courage these qualities make for unambitious and overly safe psychotherapy. I believe that therapists without courage ultimately lack the wherewithal to help clients with difficult problems, especially when those clients tax the clinical relationship. I will describe several key areas in which the lack of therapist courage serves our clients poorly.

The first area is psychotherapy with men who are not very interested in psychotherapy. Therapy, after all, is a world of feelings and introspection and vulnerability, a world that is often alien to the traditional culture of masculinity. As a result, many men darken a therapist's doorway only when their marriage or family is in deep trouble. In the first session of couples therapy, these men are often confused, angry, unconnected to their feelings, competitive with the therapists, and skeptical that therapy can help. Hardly a therapist's delight in the early going.

I have seen too many therapists excuse such a man from couples therapy on the grounds that "each spouse should work separately on their personal issues." The therapist offers to continue to do individual treatment with the wife—the good client—and refers the husband to a colleague. The husband goes once or twice, or not at all, while the wife continues in therapy. The therapist justifies this approach on clinical grounds, but I think an underlying dynamic in many cases is lack of confidence in dealing with a distant, angry man who is unsocialized into the world of psychotherapy. The result typically is that he does not get help, she gets comforting and personal growth but little help with her marriage, and she concludes that his lack of follow-through in his own therapy is a sign of his failure as a husband. And the therapist has successfully rationalized his or her own discomfort in dealing with difficult men and with the hot conflict that often occurs in marital therapy. In some cases, I believe the marriage is a casualty of the therapist's limited courage.

Clearly, not every situation calls for couples therapy. And sometimes the therapist is not trained in couples therapy, so courage is not the issue as much as competence. But I believe there are too many therapists who are instinctively drawn to the gentler world of psychotherapy with women and with therapy-savvy men and intimidated by the more difficult work with therapy-naive men, especially angry, skeptical men. (Of course, there are also many difficult female clients, as well as difficult male clients who are therapy-savvy.)

The main problem here is not that some therapists have difficulty working with these men (we all have clients we have trouble working with), but that they see the obstacle as lying in their potential clients rather than in themselves. As a result, they make clinical recommendations designed to treat their own anxiety rather than the client's problems. Now there is nothing wrong with taking care of our own anxiety—and with declining to work with clients who bother us too much. What is wrong, clinically and ethically, is not taking responsibility for how our own insecurities influence our clinical decisions. This failure of nerve serves clients poorly and undermines the moral integrity of therapy and the therapist.

Nothing scares therapists more than the threat of a client suicide. It is considered the ultimate clinical failure, an experience seared into the memory of every therapist who has experienced it. We play and replay what happened for weeks or months afterward. Nowadays the pain is twofold: the loss of a client in this tragic way, and the fear of litigation. In this era when self-responsibility seems an antiquated Victorian notion, more families are apt to fault the therapist for the suicide of their loved one. It is therefore becoming increasingly difficult for therapists to practice the virtue of courage when a client talks about suicide. Our colleagues and our attorneys urge caution and careful documentation; less often do they support taking risks that might enhance the sense of autonomy and interpersonal support for the client who does not clearly need to be in the hospital.

The result, I believe, is unnecessary use of hospitalization of suicidal clients in order to treat the anxiety of the therapist. In nonsuicide clinical situations, therapists' lack of courage is most often shown in lack of intervention. (For example, I could have stayed out of the relationship between Lorraine and Dr. Murphy.) With suicide, lack of courage is generally shown in too much intervention too soon—in the form of a therapist-initiated hospitalization of a client who could be responsibly treated as an outpatient if the therapist mobilized family and other support systems and worked more intensively with the client through the crisis. Sometimes a reluctant client agrees to be hospitalized when the therapist makes a persuasive case for it, sometimes the client is hospitalized involuntarily, and sometimes the therapist implicitly threatens to terminate treatment unless the client goes to the hospital.

I certainly believe that the hospital is where some suicidal clients need to be; I have treated acutely suicidal people who almost certainly would not be alive now if they had not been hospitalized. But I believe that many hospitalizations occur either prematurely or for inadequate reasons because the therapist flinches at the thought of treating someone at risk of self-destruction. The therapist then passes the ball to the hospital, which has its own set of economic incentives to offer inpatient treatment.

I have witnessed this tendency in all kinds of cases, but particularly with adolescents who make suicide gestures. Usually the adolescent is already past the crisis by the time he or she begins a six-month hospital stay, followed by generally inadequate resources for outpatient therapy. The therapist hears the "s" word, panics, and calls the hospital; the hospital can get reimbursed on grounds of medical necessity because the adolescent has made a suicide attempt (often a nonlethal call for attention and help). The adolescent now carries a major league psychiatric label, the insurance company or the family foots a major league bill, and the professionals involved have protected themselves from criticism and litigation. Sometimes, of course, hospitalization may have provided the best care possible. But in some cases, I believe, the decision stems from a lack of "firmness of spirit" in facing the gravest of threats in the realm of psychotherapy.

The next case ended in a necessary hospitalization, but it was a single hospitalization instead of several, and one based on the client's decision instead of the therapist's fears.

Bill tested my mettle more severely than any other suicidal client I have had. Aged forty-five and married to Cynthia, aged thirty-eight, Bill had been in and out of depressions for much of his adult life. Ten years prior to seeing me, he had been involuntarily hospitalized by his former wife, an experience he found humiliating and utterly without benefit. He came to see me for psychological help in dealing with a heart condition that was treatable but often debilitating. He was holding on to his job but needed frequent days off. I decided to work with him and his wife together—interspersed with individual sessions with Bill—because their marriage and family (two small children) were increasingly becoming dominated by his physical problems and his depression and because his marriage was the most positive element in Bill's life. Bill had been on medication for his depressive symptoms for many years.

In a private session early in the therapy, Bill told me he was starting to think about killing himself, that he had lots of ways to do it (he wouldn't tell me what they were), but that he would not go through with it at this point because of his concerns for his children and his wife. As we talked, I underlined his sense of obligation to his family, and I urged him to view suicide, although attractive as an escape from his painful life, as being "not an option," given his responsibilities in life. He liked the phrase "not an option" and began using it himself. I told him that, as his therapist, I needed him to be honest with me when he was suicidal so that we could discuss his situation. He agreed but said he would be honest with me about his suicidal thoughts or plans only if I agreed to never commit him to a mental hospital. He said that the last time was so horrible that he had vowed to kill himself for sure if he were involuntarily committed again.

I agreed to this pact with Bill: he would be honest with me, and I would not call 911 on him, unless he was jumping out a window in front of me. I accepted this arrangement because I believed it was in Bill's best interest to maintain a sense of control of his life and because I thought it was the only way he could trust me. I knew I was limiting my options when he became suicidal again and that I could be second-guessed if he ended up dead. But after considerable reflection and consultation with a colleague, agreeing to the pact seemed the right thing to do for Bill's therapy. All previous attempts to rescue him had only made things worse.

Months later, Bill was deteriorating physically and emotionally. The therapy was difficult, but I had a good relationship with Bill and Cynthia. Bill brought up suicide again during a session but assured me and his wife that he would not act on his thoughts. I wasn't sure he was leveling with me at this point, and he was becoming more agitated. A few days later, I had a phone message from Bill. He rarely called, and so I was concerned. Instead of waiting until the end of the day to call back, I did so between sessions. Sounding agitated but coherent, Bill told me that he had taken what he believed was a lethal dose of his antidepressant medication thirty minutes before and that he had called to follow through on his promise to be honest with me about the issue of suicide and to ask me to explain things to his wife.

This was the moment that tested my promise to not call 911 on him. I decided to try to convince him to allow me to call the ambulance for him. Taking an empathetic but authoritative stance, I borrowed a line from my colleague Noel Larson when I told Bill that I didn't think he was in the right frame of mind to make such a big decision. I noted that he clearly had made suicide an option again for himself and that I respected his right to decide his own fate. But I could not accept a decision made when he was so out of sorts. His determination softened as we continued talking. I then asked him for his permission to call an ambulance. He argued that things would never get better even if he lived. I replied that perhaps he was right, and that I would be willing to talk with him about whether his life was worth living, but that for now he was not in the right frame of mind for such a final decision. I again asked for his permission to call the ambulance. He agreed. I asked him to stay on the line until I got back on it. I called the ambulance and talked with Bill until it arrived.

Bill experienced this hospitalization very differently from his past one, in large part, I believe, because I had stayed the course with him and let him make the decision. I don't know what I would have done if he had not given me permission to call the ambulance; perhaps I would have called the ambulance, and I would certainly have called his wife. The moment of courage (again, retrospectively) was my willingness to not pull the plug on his right to make his own decision about living or dying. In the face of an overdose gradually taking its effect, I supported his autonomy, wasting precious minutes of rescue time, minutes I would have had difficulty defending in court if they had been crucial for his survival:

ATTORNEY: Dr. Doherty, were you or were you not aware that your client had taken a potentially lethal dose of medication?

ME: I was aware.

ATTORNEY: And were you aware that time was of the essence in order to prevent irreversible physical damage from occurring to your client?

ME: Yes, I was.

ATTORNEY: Could you explain to the court why you engaged in an extended conversation, during which time your client passed out and could not be revived by the ambulance team?

ME: I felt it was important that he be the one to make the decision to call an ambulance, and I had promised not to call 911 if he told me he was suicidal.

ATTORNEY: I see. Is this the standard of care in your professional community?

ME: I guess not.

ATTORNEY: No further questions.

I'm glad I did not have to face this court proceeding, because the most cautious course is generally the one that is ethically and legally the safest. Obstetricians get sued for not doing cesarean section deliveries far more often than for doing them. When the outcome is poor, courage and risk-taking look foolish. Bill survived and later prospered in therapy. A boil was lanced during this crisis, and he and I had a powerful clinical bond: he knew for certain that I would treat him as an agent of his own life.

A quality is a virtue only if it is hard to practice consistently. Every virtue has two negative sides: the tendency to exaggerate it and the tendency to underplay it. Exaggerated courage is foolhardiness based on poor judgment. (See chapter 8 for further discussion of this point.) Here I will discuss another negative side of courage, the one traditionally called "cowardice," an even more antiquated term than courage. Cowardice connotes running away from a fight, which actually can be a prudent act in many situations. Young men who avoided the Vietnam War on grounds of conscience were often dubbed cowards when many were brave in their resistance. Because I think the word *coward* carries too much baggage to be retrieved, I generally use expressions like "lack of courage," "lapse of courage," or "failure of nerve." But they all mean "cowardly."

Every human being has experienced those moments when we stood still or retreated when we knew we should have gone ahead. I reserve for the category of cowardice my response to those situations in which I know what I ought to do, I know that I have the ability to do it, but I fail to act because of fear of dealing with conflict or some other troubling but manageable obstacle—in other words, when I chicken out of something I am capable of doing and believe I should do.

In chapter 4, I described the case of Nathan, the man who was lying to his wife about his ominous medical condition. I leaned on him at first to tell her and said that I could not be an ally with his secret. But when he pleaded with me to give him time, I had a failure of nerve. Nathan was a very angry man who not infrequently scared me. When he became agitated during a session, he would sometimes pick up a hard-edged piece of decorative glass and toss it back and forth between one hand and the other. I sometimes had the fantasy that the glass would make a very large dent in the middle of my forehead.

I was reasonably brave during the sessions when Nathan was angry at me. I remained nonreactive and helped him focus his anger where it belonged. But when he appealed to my pity—and also implicitly threatened to become nasty if I did not comply with his wishes—I retreated. Retreating in that session may have been prudent, since I did not want to coerce him into telling his wife about his heart condition. He needed time to think about it. But my backing away completely from the issue in the subsequent sessions stemmed almost entirely from my lapse of courage. When he did not bring up the issue himself in couples sessions, I knew he was going to keep it secret. I should have met with him alone to confront him, but I played along, largely, I believe in retrospect, to avoid confrontation. Perhaps it would not have worked, but I owed it to him and to myself as a therapist to raise an uncomfortable issue that was undermining the therapy. At the time, I rationalized my decision by telling myself that I was being flexible and not imposing my own rules on this client. But now I see my actions as lacking the "firmness of spirit" to do the right thing by my client.

Compounding the failure of courage in situations like this is not facing your cowardly deed honestly. In fact, facing ourselves honestly might be the essential form of courage for psychotherapists, because that is what we are asking our clients to do. The dangerous therapists are not the ones who recognize and feel badly about their failure to take an appropriate risk, but the ones who rationalize their lapses or put the responsibility on the clients. I could have told myself, for example, that because Nathan would not be able to do anything constructive with my challenge, my inaction was really his fault, or I could have labeled it a prudent strategy. I would have been lying to myself.

Recognizing and confronting our own emotional reactions to our clients—termed countertransference in psychodynamic therapy—is a special form of courage required of therapists more than of any other group of professionals. The reason is that, of all the helping professions, we have arguably the most intense relationships with our clients. Just as a surgeon dealing with a life-threatening emergency must act with a special kind of courage, therapists are called to be brave about their inner lives as they affect the practice of therapy. Failure of nerve in this area is bound to harm our clients because we will not be able to really see and understand them through the invisible veil of our distortions.

Looking steadily at ourselves in the mirror, then, is the special form of therapeutic courage that enables us to take risks with clients. If I had done this better in working with Nathan, I would have realized why I was not confronting him, and then I would probably have taken action. Many failures of nerve by therapists can be traced back to flinching from self-awareness.[4]

As with acts of physical courage, major acts of courage in therapy happen only when therapists practice everyday courage in facing more routine challenges. Will the client fire me for pushing for less punitive child discipline techniques? Will the client leave— and tell his or her friends—if I persist in challenging destructive behavior? If I question my client's abuse of a community system— tax cheating, corporate ripoffs, welfare fraud—will I be dismissed as a meddling do-gooder? If I try to tame a squabbling couple who are acting like two-year-olds in my office, will they turn on me? Therapists are people who like to be close to others and important to them; that's partly why we go into this business. And that's why our timidity can sometimes be rationalized as acceptance, nurturance, and caring. Both good and mediocre therapists give large doses of acceptance, nurturance, and caring; the best therapists are also brave enough to make clients uncomfortable at times and to risk therapeutic closeness by plunging into murky waters their more circumspect colleagues would avoid.

Courage is also needed outside the therapy room when therapists see their colleagues engage in unethical or potentially destructive behavior toward clients. Sometimes therapists know or suspect that a colleague has been involved sexually with a client or is psychologically impaired and making poor clinical judgments, but they do not speak up to the therapist or anyone else. These are extraordinarily challenging moments for therapists, especially in the current litigious climate; an aggrieved colleague might threaten legal action against an "accuser" who is acting responsibly and bravely.

Assertive action toward larger systems, such as insurance companies, can be even riskier than challenging colleagues. Therapists sometimes feel that their clients are being treated unjustly by third-party payers, such as when a client is deprived of essential therapy visits or jerked around from one therapist to another when the client's company changes insurance providers. Sometimes the insurance company or managed care reviewers grant a limited number of sessions with no review but then expect the client to be in very serious trouble to merit more sessions. Sometimes therapists request more sessions and then have not only the request denied but the first set of sessions disapproved retroactively, with the therapist footing the bill. Some therapists fear that if they attract too much attention to their practices, the managers of mental health reimbursement might decide to drop them from the panel of approved providers, or worse, audit their caseload and retroactively deny reimbursement on many of their cases, thereby effectively bankrupting the therapist, who has to pay it all back. As a result of these perceived threats, some therapists refuse to request more sessions for a client, even if the client needs them. When therapists reach the point—and many have—where advocacy for clients seems self-destructive, then psychotherapy as a healing profession is seriously compromised. Collective acts of courage become a moral imperative.

I take inspiration from the courage of my close associates, and I find it useful to use the term "courage" explicitly when it seems to fit their behavior. A colleague, for instance, agreed to testify against the criminally abusive husband of a client, even though the husband had threatened the therapist and somehow acquired her home address. As one of the consultants in this case, I recognized the anguish of the therapist while she struggled about her legitimate fear for her own safety and her genuine concern for her client—and for the rest of society, which has to deal with violent men like this one. I certainly could not prescribe the morally correct decision: when is the risk too great to take on behalf of a client? My colleague ultimately decided to testify, an act I regarded as genuinely heroic, one involving extraordinary courage in the face of serious risks to herself. I myself have never faced such a decision, and I would have respected her decision either way. But I found it uplifting to frame her action as one of great courage, not just as one of great caring (which it was) or great public service (which it also was). What she did was brave beyond the normal expectations of therapists.

In addition to being exemplars, colleagues serve the essential role of supporting us when we take risks in therapy. I could not have gotten through my experience with Lorraine and Dr. Murphy had it not been for the support and advice of my colleague. I would either have wilted under the pressure or, more likely, defended my actions clumsily and defensively, thereby undermining the helpfulness of my risky initiative. With my trusted colleague behind me, I felt like I was doing cotherapy. Colleagues are particularly important when we are considering confronting another professional; they can help us sort out our reasons and bolster our self-confidence in taking on a peer we think is out of line. The bottom line is that courage, like all the other virtues, is developed and practiced in interpersonal contexts. Each profession has special qualities of courage required of it. Ours is work of the heart, for which we need regular transfusions of support and challenge from our close colleagues.

Courage in facing threats from outside therapy also needs group support. Acting alone, most therapists will keep their heads low, out of the line of fire, and will not forcefully challenge unjust policies and practices. They will work the edges of ethical compromise, for example, by slightly exaggerating the severity of the mental health diagnosis in order for the client to get treatment, by concealing a personality disorder diagnosis that will signal the third-party payer not to approve more treatment, or by disguising marital therapy as "individual therapy with spouse present."

Often the utilization reviewers know the therapists are playing a game for the benefit of the client and look the other way if the request for services does not appear unreasonable. Psychotherapy, after all, is not an exact science.

Thus evolves a series of small ethical compromises serving the function of eroding the therapist's moral leverage to resist unfair practices and policies. It is only by organizing into groups that therapists can hope to receive support for making courageous individual stands and to conceive joint action that has a chance of bringing about change. The postscript to this book describes a plan for groups that could provide mutual support and organized action to preserve the ethical integrity of psychotherapy in a world where market forces and government regulation increasingly sterilize this healing art and where therapists' own collusion has contributed mightily to the problem.

No rules come out of this analysis of courage, no prescriptions for how to act bravely and avoid lapses of courage. But the small acts of courage of everyday practice—confronting someone when we'd just as soon leave the issue alone for now, being honest with ourselves about our internal reactions and personal issues as they come up, refusing to blame clients for our mistakes, advocating for clients with their insurance companies—these everyday acts of courage prepare us for the big challenges of suicide, serious conflict with other professionals, the erosion of therapeutic practice in the face of market forces, and threats to our own emotional and physical safety. Firmness of spirit is an acquired virtue that as therapists we are called to embrace and cultivate throughout our careers, for the good of our clients and the community, and for the enrichment of our own humanity.

CHAPTER 8

Prudence

THE ANCIENT GREEKS CONSIDERED PRUDENCE THE MASTER virtue because it regulates all the others. Courage without prudence leads to danger and death, caring without prudence leads to invasions of autonomy, truthfulness without prudence leads to tactless hurts, and community service without prudence leads to neglect of one's personal world. An old-fashioned but evocative term, prudence in contemporary parlance refers to good judgment or, in the words of *Merriam-Webster*, "a quality in a person that allows [him or her] to choose a sensible course of action." Common sense, if you will, backed up by wisdom.

Why put prudence on the short list of key virtues for psychotherapists? Because therapists must make so many clinical decisions every day that are "judgment calls" not backed by any scientific or clinical certainty, and because we serve as consultants to our clients about so many life decisions made in similar conditions of uncertainty. A mark of a very good therapist is the ability to consistently make the right move at the right time. These therapists are sought after for consultation by their colleagues, not just because of their knowledge and technical skills but because they have a fine sense of judgment. When they tell us we are in trouble, we listen. When they ask why we are playing it safe, we reevaluate our case. Prudence rightly understood is not about being cautious but about being wise.

When I think about imprudent actions by a therapist, I recall one of my early marital therapy cases. Dorothy and Howard, a couple in their midthirties with a daughter age seven, came into therapy at Howard's request. Dorothy had announced to Howard that she had been very unhappy for some time and that she was fed up with the marriage. Contributing to this realization was an affair she had, but the affair was now over. Howard was very active in the first therapy session, pressing his case for her to stay and try to revive the marriage. He was willing to change, he said. Dorothy, on the other hand, appeared quietly distressed and was not very forthcoming about what she wanted to do.

I had recently learned the principle in couples therapy that you must have an agreement from both parties to work on the relationship, a commitment to work on the relationship in therapy, in order to learn whether a commitment to the marriage is sustainable. Too much couples work, I had discovered, bogged down in the marshes of ambivalence over whether to work on the problems or move toward separating. I therefore pressed Dorothy to decide what she wanted. I explained my position that I could help them split up constructively or I could help them try to salvage their marriage, but I needed each of them to vote on which option they wanted me to work with them on. She kept saying she wasn't sure. I explored her ambivalence, but she offered little insight into what was going on inside her. We were at a stalemate as the session ended, and we agreed to meet the next week, at which time I said I would try to help Dorothy make her decision.

This recounting of the session probably underplays the degree of compassion I showed to Dorothy, as well as the other marital issues we explored constructively, but it accurately reflects my memory of my assertive stance on moving past her ambivalence. Prior to the next session, Howard called to tell me that they would not be coming back to therapy because, although he thought it was a very constructive session, Dorothy had felt pushed too hard. I asked to speak to Dorothy, who confirmed what he said. I apologized and urged them to come back at least once more to see if we could work this out. She declined. I gave them the names of several colleagues they could see for further therapy. I felt terrible, because I realized Dorothy was right about my actions.

I was guilty of poor judgment, or lack of prudence, in this case. I pushed ahead vigorously when I should have stayed with her in her ambivalence. I should have guessed, for example, that although she was not being open in front of Howard, she might have been more forthcoming about her feelings and intentions if I talked with her alone. Maybe he was beating her, maybe she had rekindled the affair, maybe she was afraid of hurting her husband with the truth that she had decided on a divorce. I had been planning to talk with her alone at the second session, but my pushy stance in the first session gave me no opportunity.

As I reflect now on this case, I recall the words of my philosophy professor, Ben Hunt, who said during a lecture, "When we learn something new, it is almost impossible not to absolutize it in some way." A new truth tends to fill the firmament for a time, blocking out older truths. The practical implication for therapists is that we may be most at risk for lapses in judgment when we have learned a sparkling new insight. This seemed true for me with Dorothy and Howard. I had crystallized an important precept of couples therapy: clarify whether you are doing decision-making work or relationship-building work. The problem was that I had put a short time frame around that clarification— decide right away, if you don't mind. I had learned an important principle but applied it wholesale at the expense of other therapeutic principles, such as sensitivity to the unique needs of the client and respect for her autonomy in making a decision only when she was ready.

I have seen therapists make some of their worst clinical mistakes after returning from a workshop with a master therapist who has well-edited clinical tapes that demonstrate marvelous new techniques. A brilliant therapy workshop on Friday afternoon spawns creative interventions galore on Monday morning. After a workshop on post-traumatic stress disorder, some therapists will see this problem in people who are merely stressed, not traumatized. Perhaps clients should be given fair warning when therapists embrace a new diagnosis or treatment technique: your therapist has learned something new and may act strangely today.

Although professional follies have a humorous side, the consequences sometimes can be grave, as when therapists begin to loosely apply a serious diagnosis (such as multiple personality disorder) and inadvertently persuade clients that they suffer from it. Some of the contemporary crisis of confidence in psychotherapy stems from the public perception that therapists are exercising poor judgment in the area of memories of childhood sexual abuse and satanic cult ritual abuse. We are accused of lacking discernment when we hear clients' stories, along with making rash conclusions about the guilty parties. In short, therapists are being roundly criticized, even ridiculed in cartoons such as "Doonesbury," for leaving their prudence at home when they go to the office.[1]

Some of this criticism, I believe, is unfair and distorted; there is a lot more abuse happening in and out of families than the public wants to acknowledge. But I believe that the "new learning" principle is operative here as well. That is, for most of the one hundred years of psychotherapy, therapists thought that childhood sexual abuse was extremely rare and they didn't believe women who were having memories or flashbacks. We have learned in the late twentieth century, in large part through the impact of feminism and the greater social awareness of abuse against children, that we missed the boat badly on a widespread social and clinical problem. This new learning, coupled with collective guilt for past ignorance, creates a fertile soil for shaky judgment. The temptation now is to believe—despite the scientific evidence on the unreliability of human memory—that every memory is literally true, every story fully believable, every accused party clearly guilty.[2]

What a difficult situation for the therapist who rejects both the old certainty (it doesn't happen) and the new certainty (if she says it happened, it happened). Some of the most prudent therapists I know take a neutral clinical stance on the historical accuracy of client memories. They work with whatever experiences the client brings to therapy, including memories of abuse, but in the absence of evidence other than the client's memory, they refrain from concluding that the parents, for example, are legally guilty of the crimes the client describes. Sometimes a client may have been psychologically abused by a parent, or physically but not sexually abused. Even if incest didn't literally happen, the feelings of victimization are fully real. What is most important, from this perspective, is to stay connected with the feelings of the client, not to make a determination of culpable responsibility.

The public outcry about the "false memory syndrome" seems based on the perception that therapists are inducing memories in clients who come to therapy for other reasons.[3] Again, I think part of the criticism is based on a wish to deny the seriousness of the problem of childhood sexual abuse in this country. But I also believe that some therapists exercise poor clinical judgment in reasoning backward from symptoms to causes, as if the presence of serious psychopathology in adult women necessarily means they were sexually abused as children, whether they remember it or not. I have heard therapists confidently make assertions such as, "Ninety-five percent of bulimic women were victims of incest." This kind of diagnostic hubris, which flies in the face of the research on the multiple pathways to bulimia and other psychological disorders, can lead the therapist to "discover" many untrue cases of incest, creating untold and unnecessary pain for the client and the family. This practice is imprudent, unwise, and incompetent therapy.[4]

What I am holding out as prudent therapy, of course, can be considered by others a cowardly cop-out from supporting women's reality. My response is that courage in the service of credulity is no virtue. And credulity is what I believe is going on with the national fixation, encouraged by therapists, on satanic cult ritual abuse. This may be the most widespread exercise of poor judgment in the history of psychotherapy, second only perhaps to our earlier poor judgment in believing that children are rarely sexually abused in their families. Therapists have become ministers of the new Salem witch-hunts.[5]

These are strong statements, so let me state my own position clearly. I believe that almost any abomination human beings can conceive has probably happened at some time, including satanic ritualistic murder and human sacrifice. In other words, any particular story might represent an actual event. What I find incredible is the notion that there are tens of thousands of such cases over the past generation in the United States, and that many of the victims are now swelling therapists' caseloads. As some critics have asked, "Where are the bones?" Why has no one reported as missing the babies who were sacrificed? Why are there no ritual scars on the living victims? Why has there been no legitimate exposé of this widespread depravity, even though any journalist, criminal investigator, or district attorney would achieve instant fame and eventual fortune for breaking the story? The only plausible answer to these questions is either that most of the reports are untrue or that there is a large-scale conspiracy, more successful by far than any other in our nation's history, to keep the satanic cult movement secret. The police detectives who investigate and find nothing must be part of the conspiracy; investigative journalists must have their own sinister reasons for not seeing the truth. The likelihood of such a conspiracy of cover-up succeeding for more than a week in a country thirsty for scatological stories—well, it strains credulity.

At a clinical level, the client with memories of satanic cult ritual abuse deserves to be treated as an individual case, not as a representative of a national trend. However unlikely, any individual client's memories might conceivably be accurate. I am not suggesting that we simply disbelieve clients with these memories. But good judgment by a professional therapist requires the ability to think epidemiologically, that is, to keep in mind the likely prevalence of certain problems in the population when making a determination about the accuracy of client memories.

Here is an illustration from the field of medicine. If a prudent pediatrician is evaluating a toddler who is overweight and eats too much, he or she is not likely to make a diagnosis of Prader Willi syndrome, since this genetic chromosomal disorder, which causes uncontrollable eating, is extremely rare in the population. Based on the epidemiology of the disorder, a primary care pediatrician should be surprised to see even one true case in a career. If this physician saw Prader Willi syndrome in a new child every month, there would be reason to suspect problems in the physician's assessment of childhood obesity. If you think you saw a zebra in your neighbor's field, it was probably a horse.

Therapists generally have not been trained in epidemiological or population-based thinking. They are trained to diagnose or assess each client as an individual, without applying baseline estimates. In most cases, this orientation works well, since the great majority of diagnoses therapists use are reasonably prevalent in the population: depression, anxiety, schizophrenia, attention deficit hyperactivity disorder, and so forth. The various editions of the *Diagnostic and Statistical Manual* of the American Psychiatric Association are not guides to rare psychiatric disorders.

This lack of an epidemiological perspective can cripple therapists' judgment when clients present stories that represent extremely rare events. If I believe all of my own clients' memories of satanic cult ritual abuse, are therapists all over my community believing similar stories? Either the phenomenon is extremely widespread (which, I believe, defies credulity) or there is a problem in how therapists are interpreting the stories clients are telling them. Clients in fact may be responding to the same cultural hysteria about satanic cults that therapists are helping to create; the syndrome may feed on its own illusions, fanned from time to time by reports of a purportedly verified case.[6]

Some therapists respond to this argument by saying that their responsibility is not to judge the accuracy of satanic abuse memories but merely to accept the reality of clients' memories. On the face of it, this sounds like the same approach I endorse for familial sexual abuse victims: do not get into juridical evaluations of evidence but accept the client's subjective experience of familial abuse. The difference is that, epidemiologically, we know that childhood sexual abuse in the home is highly prevalent in U.S. society and that it is likely to be part of the history of many psychotherapy patients. Therefore, the accuracy of such memories is plausible, if not always provable because of the limitations of long-term memories. And many therapists are active in public efforts to expose and prevent childhood sexual abuse. In other words, sexual abuse is a bona fide clinical, public health, and criminal justice problem that nevertheless requires careful clinical judgment in each case.

With satanic cult ritual abuse, we have a syndrome whose prevalence is unknown and hotly contested. Therefore, I believe it is not enough to focus only on my private clients and deny my responsibility as a member of the community to make a judgment about whether we are facing a frightening epidemic of murder and torture by satanic cults. The advocates for cult victims are at least being consistent in blowing the whistle as loud as they can through professional conferences and the media. Less consistent are the majority of therapists who believe all their individual clients but suspend judgment about how widespread the problem is—even though they know that thousands of therapists are seeing the same kinds of clients and coming to similar conclusions. This is a failure of judgment that I consider a breakdown in professional responsibility, one in the same league with therapists' historical failure to recognize childhood sexual abuse as a widespread phenomenon.

This lapse in judgment is creating an atmosphere among therapists that is leading some to embrace what may be the next national hysteria: UFO aliens kidnapping and brainwashing earthlings. There are already well-known mental health professionals sounding the alarm and making this diagnosis in troubled people who come to therapy. If we do not get our act together soon about what constitutes prudent clinical judgment, I fear that our fellow citizens will recoil from everything psychotherapists touch, as they eventually did with the Salem witch-hunts, and psychotherapy may become less attractive to people, including those with bizarre memories of victimization who badly need the help. When "Doonesbury" discovers therapists' attraction to alien kidnappings, it might be time to lower the sails and ride out the storm.

If 80 percent of life is showing up, most of the rest is timing. A sense of timing is the hallmark of the prudent therapist. I am reminded of the Kenny Rogers song about "The Gambler" who "knows when to hold 'em, and knows when to fold 'em, knows when to walk away, and knows when to run." Therapists make hundreds of small clinical decisions each day about timing: when to support, when to challenge, when to probe, when to reflect, when to pursue an issue, when to let it lie, when to offer an interpretation, when to be silent. More global are the decisions about the timing of major interventions: when to hold a whole-family session, when to see family members individually, when to talk to the referring physician, when to move on from one behavioral exercise to the next, when to refer for medication, when to move toward closure of the therapy. The list is almost endless.

Good timing is at the heart of good therapy, exquisite timing is at the heart of great therapy, and poor timing, I believe, is one of the most common ingredients in poor therapy. The following case illustrates the importance of the timing of interpretations about the underlying dynamics in clients' lives.

Michael, age 19, had been in and out of mental hospitals since the age of sixteen for treatment of severe depression and occasional alcohol abuse. I became involved in the case when his mother, Joan, came to see me for individual help dealing with the breakup of her relationship with a man. She and Michael's father had been divorced for many years; he lived far away and had sporadic contact with Michael. During the first session, I noticed that Joan was carrying a beeper. When I inquired about it, she said it was for Michael to use to be able to reach her at any time. Michael, it turns out, was in the locked ward of a mental hospital and called his mother when he had complaints about the staff.

Halfway through the session, Joan's beeper went off. She asked if she could make the call from my office, picked up the phone, and placed the call. Joan listened to Michael's complaints about the hospital, tried to comfort him, and told him that she would take prompt action to try either to have him switched to another hospital or to be released in the care of a different psychiatrist whom Michael liked. After ten minutes on the phone, Joan returned to our discussion and told me about Michael's history. When I offered to help Joan in this area of her life, she readily took me up on the offer.

The next week Joan arrived with Michael, who had been released from the hospital. Michael was a tall young man with the demeanor of a thirteen-year-old. Joan did almost all the talking for him, although he responded intelligently when I asked him questions. He was clearly a very disturbed young man—anorexically thin, on multiple psychoactive medications, and unsure of his ability to function in daily life. Michael had done reasonably well as a child until his midteens, around the time of his parents' divorce, when his first bout of depression occurred, followed by suicide attempts and repeated hospitalizations. He had graduated from high school along the way and was a brilliant student when he was able to focus his attention. His siblings lived out of state and had limited contact with him.

Michael, who lived with his mother, had very little autonomy in thought or behavior. Joan had the psychiatrist's home phone and called frequently to discuss Michael's situation—an intrusion that angered Michael and sometimes precipitated his acting out through his symptoms. Once, when Michael had a girlfriend for a brief period of time, Joan insisted on trying to become the girl's friend too. Michael just retreated.

It did not take a diagnostic genius to see this as a highly over-involved or enmeshed mother-son relationship that was probably perpetuating Michael's problems and keeping him from becoming an adult. This realization had not been lost on the plethora of therapists who had worked with them over the years. At one point, I met the current group of nurses and therapists during one of Michael's hospitalizations and was struck with their hostility toward his mother. They expressed fantasies of rescuing Michael from her, implying that if Joan would only back off, Michael might have a chance in life.

All the therapists agreed, then, that the extraordinarily enmeshed mother-son relationship was a key element in the case. Where we differed was in our sense of timing in challenging Joan about her overinvolvement. For five years, therapists and hospital staff had regularly communicated to Joan that she was over-responsible and intrusive and recommended that she back off and let them take care of Michael. When these interventions elicited nothing but fear and defensiveness from Joan, they worked on Michael to try to get him to distance from his mother. Their efforts were met with agreement from Michael that his mother was controlling and intrusive, but his ambivalent moves toward freedom generally took irresponsible forms—such as disappearing for a day or two—that served to increase Joan's anxiety and monitoring behavior. At one point, after a psychiatrist told Michael point-blank that he had to drastically curtail his contact with his mother if he ever wanted to be healthy, Michael ended up back in the hospital after making another suicide attempt.

This family was suffering from lack of prudent timing on the part of mental health professionals. Applying a simplistic medical model, the professionals were identifying a major problem, pointing it out to the patient and his mother, and then intervening directly to alleviate the problem. And they were making things worse.

I took a much slower and more supportive stance toward Joan's relationship with Michael. I heard in Joan's stories of the past five years how often she had been the only one who sensed that Michael was nearing a breakdown or that he was not going to respond to a particular form of therapy. Joan in fact knew her son far better than any therapist did. She knew when he was lying to the medical team, she knew when he was pretending to take his antidepressant medications, and, most important, she could sense when Michael might be contemplating a suicide attempt. Here was a mother, then, with a seriously ill son whose life she had saved on a number of occasions, a son who was frequently not honest with his psychiatrists and therapists. Joan's own family history of abandonment by her mother and her difficulties with self-worth and interpersonal boundaries, combined with her son's problems, made a volatile—and life-threatening—mixture that required extreme prudence and delicacy by any therapist.

From the outset, I resisted referring to Joan's actions as overprotective of her son, even when Joan brought up the topic by saying something like, "I think Dr. Osborne believes I am the cause of Michael's problems because I overprotect him and smother him." I would first toss the question back to Joan, who would defend herself, and then I would express my sympathy for how difficult it must have been over the years to be called overprotective when she believed her son would not have lived without her monitoring. Parents with seriously ill children have to protect and watch more than other parents, and it's hard to say where the proper line is between healthy monitoring and overprotection. Most of us as parents instinctively would rather err on the side of caution. When I made these kinds of statements to Joan, I was not being disingenuous; I truly believe them. But there was more to the story than I thought Joan was able to hear at that point. Dealing explicitly with her overinvolvement would have elicited a terrific shame reaction from her, followed by no constructive change and a breach in my clinical relationship with her. Instead, I worked pragmatically to help her deal with everyday autonomy issues with Michael, who also attended most of the therapy sessions. I was helping them build boundaries without implying that the past boundaries were anyone's fault.

After one of Michael's most serious suicide attempts, I was able to get him involved with a new individual therapist, a highly skilled colleague who could understand both his desire for autonomy and his ambivalence about it. Joan trusted this therapist because of my recommendation and was able to accept the therapist's tight boundary around her clinical relationship with Michael. No more phone conversations between Mom and the therapist about Michael's treatment. From this point onward, despite one more life-threatening setback, Michael's progress was rapid.

After Michael was out of clinical danger, had moved to a college dorm fifty miles away, and was doing extremely well in school and making new friends, Joan was able to relax enough to contemplate more directly her prior level of overinvolvement with her son. We were able to put this relationship into the context of others in her life, for example, her difficulty holding her own in relationships with men, starting with her father, and her tendency to hurt her relationships with women by being too intense too soon. Defying the predictions of many prior therapists who had suggested that Joan would fall apart once her son became emotionally emancipated, Joan began to thrive. She focused more on her job, which she had been in danger of losing, and started a new, healthier relationship with a man.

There was a lot more to this case than good timing, of course, and my therapist colleague no doubt deserves more credit than I do for Michael's near-miraculous turnaround. But without a prudent sense of what to say and when—and what to keep quiet about—the path would never have been cleared for Michael and Joan to find their way to separate but connected and healthy lives.

Michael and Joan's case was one of those success stories in which major change occurred in the clients' lives. Prudence is also reflected in the ability to accept the limits of the changes that can be achieved in psychotherapy. The cases we read about in books or see on video are generally the raving successes and the total cures—or, at best, cases in which a moderate degree of change was achieved against great odds. The resulting socialization of therapists can seduce us into poor judgment about what we are able to accomplish in therapy and what clients should be willing to settle for in their lives. We sometimes imprudently expect too much of ourselves and our clients. The next case serves as a bookend to Dorothy and Howard's case, in which I pushed too hard for clarity of commitment, and illustrates the paradoxical power of accepting the inability to change.

Dick and Mary had a long courtship marked by Dick's indecisiveness about whether to get married. During this time, Mary moved around the country to various jobs in her field; Dick visited her during his vacations, and they saw each other when Mary returned to her hometown for family visits. Finally, after Mary became pregnant during one of their times together, she gave him an ultimatum, and he agreed to get married right away. When they came to see me, their son was two years old, Dick was a devoted stay-at-home dad who did occasional manual labor jobs, and Mary worked as a lawyer.

They came to see me at Mary's initiative because both were unhappy in the marriage. She was committed to the relationship but was having problems with his criticism of her and his ambivalence about staying married. Dick admitted criticizing Mary for her appearance and personal habits—she was too heavy, he thought, and too disorganized—but most of all he had doubts about whether this marriage was for him. What kept him going every day was his attachment to his son and his fondness for Mary. He was willing to work on the relationship to see if it could be satisfactory, but he said he had always had problems making decisions about relationships.

We worked first on their interpersonal boundaries, particularly Dick's tendency to monitor Mary's food intake and exercise patterns; I helped them understand the unhealthiness of her trying to live by his standards for her. We moved on to work on improving their problem-solving skills (they tended to avoid disagreements). The therapy was not easy, but they made steady improvement. Mary was feeling much better, and Dick could see that life was smoother when he respected her autonomy and spoke up for himself in legitimate areas, such as his concern about her overly busy work schedule.

When I revisited the commitment issue, Dick had not moved a bit. However, he was able to be more honest about his regret that he had made the decision to get married under pressure. I took more history on Dick's life before Mary. His father had died when Dick was eight, leaving him with his mother and a younger sister. As the oldest child and only boy, he immediately became the man of the house for his mother. One of his memories after his father's funeral was getting out the big lawnmower and cutting the grass by himself, with his mother weeding the garden nearby. He and his mother became very tight, and when he began to date years later, she never liked any girl he became involved with. She particularly disliked Mary when her son became strongly attached to her and hated to see him move away with Mary. Dick's frequently expressed desire to move back to his home state was one of the ongoing sticking points in the marriage.

This information was right out of Psychotherapy 101. An early parental loss followed by an undifferentiated relationship with his mother had left Dick chronically ambivalent about commitment and intimacy. He was willing to explore these issues, but in several individual sessions his level of understanding of himself stayed intellectual. He would say, "That sounds reasonable, but I don't know how that helps me decide whether to stay or leave."

When he told me his mother was coming to town for a visit, I asked him to invite her to a session. His mother had acquired a lot of insight into what she considered her mistakes in raising Dick to be so close to her. She told him she hoped he could commit himself to Mary, whom she now liked. Dick took in his mother's opinion in his usual intellectual way, like an engineer learning historical information about why a bridge was unsturdy but remaining clueless as how to use the information to make the bridge stronger. He was a fairly content man whose only significant problem, he believed, was lifelong ambivalence about his relationships with women. He fantasized about a previous lover but realized that he would probably have commitment problems with her if he left Mary and joined her. Furthermore, he could not imagine living away from his little boy. Dick, perhaps influenced by the loss of his own father, did parental commitment very well.

When I reassembled Mary and Dick to evaluate where to go with the therapy, they reported they were getting along much better. The remaining problem, a potentially relationship-ending one, was Dick's inability to say that he was committed to the marriage permanently. After a lot of consultation with colleagues, I had given up trying to help Dick break through his ambivalence. When I summarized how I saw their impasse they both looked at me with concern and asked, "Where do we go from here?"

This was a moment when I could have framed Dick's lack of commitment as a fatal flaw in the relationship, moving at that point to support the idea that Mary had the right to such commitment. Dick would have become more rigid in making what I call the Popeye defense—"I yam what I yam"—and their relationship could have deteriorated badly, with my principled assistance, of course. After all, I had learned that commitment is the cornerstone of a marriage; without it, there is nothing to work with.

Instead of moving in the direction of confrontation, however, I opened the door to acceptance. Turning to Mary, I observed that she obviously had a good man here (she had said as much), somebody who loved her, supported her in her work, and was an equal partner at home and a devoted father. But he had a personal problem with ambivalence. He understood where it came from but was unable, at this point in his life, to overcome it. She had to decide whether to stay married to Dick knowing that he was unable now, and maybe permanently, to say the words "I want to stay married to you forever" or to accept his everyday attitude and behavior as commitment enough for her, despite the lack of words. She reckoned she could accept Dick, limitations and all, because she was happy with their everyday life and because he in fact acted like he was committed to her.

I next turned to Dick and said that his problem with ambivalence about commitment was one that he had struggled with but was apparently unable to overcome at this point. He had learned that the issue wasn't about his relationship with Mary in particular but about commitment to any woman. Since he might remain ambivalent all his life, the question for Dick to ponder was whether Mary was the woman he wanted to be ambivalent with. Within a few minutes, the whole issue was transformed. Mary did not have to see herself as compromising her self-worth by settling for an uncommitted husband; Dick was in reality very committed but unable to admit it. Dick did not have to see himself as throwing away his future happiness by settling for an ambivalent relationship instead of some other fully committed relationship. His ambivalence was like a chronic knee problem that would hamper him somewhat in any sport he played. Why not play the sport he loved?

Five years later, Mary and Dick were still together and still doing well. They taught me something important about the wisdom of accepting what cannot be changed, without a sense of tragedy or failure. If they had had the misfortune to come to me as a therapist early in my career, I might have insisted on teaching them a lesson about not settling for a car whose engine is not firing on all the pistons. Some of my change no doubt stems from personal maturation—accepting my own limits and those of people I love and learning to live graciously with problems that don't go away. But the other part of my change stems from a deeper appreciation of the importance of maintaining commitments to "good-enough" relationships that carry history and roots and responsibilities instead of discarding them in the quest for the holy grail of the perfect relationship.

The case of Mary and Dick illustrates the importance of prudent judgment by therapists when people in our care are making life-changing decisions. Notice that I was not prescriptive—I did not tell them they should stay together. What I did was offer a way to frame their difficulty that left them each an opening to maintain their satisfactory marriage without selling out their needs and integrity as individuals.

Therapists have enormous influence through the way they frame questions and make observations with clients. One of my early clinical teachers used to say, when I was scared about making mistakes as a novice therapist, that it is at least as hard to really harm a client as it is to really help a client. That idea was comforting, but I no longer believe it. Perhaps it's true for the routine moments of therapy, but at those bracketed moments of moral intensity in people's lives, we have the power to help and harm in equal measure. That is why (to paraphrase a New Testament discussion of the virtues), though we have caring, truthfulness, courage, and service to community—and all the training one could dream of—if we have not prudence, we have nothing.

Postscript: Finding a Good Therapist and Creating Moral Communities Among Therapists

I HAVE ARGUED THAT MANY WELL-TRAINED THERAPISTS hold a worldview that blinds them to issues of moral responsibility in their clients' lives and deemphasizes the character of the therapist and the needs of the larger community. I have also argued that therapists who are open to these issues are well situated to provide moral consultation along with traditional psychotherapy. So how do you choose a morally sensitive therapist? This is a question for therapists and nontherapists alike, since therapists themselves refer many people to other therapists and frequently seek out therapy for themselves. Therapists may advertise their credentials and clinical specialty areas, but they don't advertise their virtues and moral sensitivity. And I wouldn't trust anyone who did.

Following are some positive qualities to look for in a morally sensitive therapist, along with warning signs to watch out for. I am assuming, of course, that the therapist you are considering (or already seeing) has appropriate professional credentials and training. Moral sensitivity is no substitute for lack of clinical competence.

What to Look for in a Good Therapist

1. *Caring*—the therapist seems genuinely compassionate and values you as a person. This sense of being cared for should start from your first contact with the therapist, whether on the phone or in the office, and should never be in serious doubt as you move through the difficult parts of therapy. I suggest trusting your intuition in the first contacts you have with the therapist. If you don't feel warmth and respect, look elsewhere.

2. *Courage*—the therapist is willing to challenge you when you are off base, even if you get angry or defensive in response. Therapy should not be just a feel-good exercise, and a therapist who does not annoy you at times is probably not doing a good job. The therapist should show you, over time if not at the outset of therapy, a willingness to persevere in facing issues that you would prefer to avoid.

3. *Prudence*—the therapist's feedback and suggestions about your life decisions seem realistic and reasonable, neither too timid nor too risky. Most good therapists are cautious about giving direct advice about a client's decisions, but when they do, the advice makes good sense, such as the classic suggestions to "sleep on it" before sending an angry letter or to not make major decisions when seriously depressed. Prudence should be visible in the first contacts with the therapist and should not flag through the course of treatment.

4. *Willingness to use moral language*—the therapist is willing to engage in moral discussion about what is fair, right, honest, or responsible. The therapist appears comfortable talking with you about your values and your religious beliefs and about your sense of right and wrong. This quality should be visible from the first time you raise these kinds of issues.

5. *Respect for your interpersonal commitments and responsibilities*—the therapist honors your inclinations to act responsibly

toward people you are committed to in your life, even when he or she is sometimes pointing out the destructive elements in these relationships. Good therapists respect their clients' pace for making difficult decisions on morally loaded decisions such as whether to divorce a spouse or whether to institutionalize an ill or disabled family member.

6. *Respect for your community commitments and responsibilities*— the therapist honors your efforts to contribute to your community, even though he or she may challenge you at times to achieve a better balance in your life. The therapist focuses not only on what your community involvement does for you but also on what it contributes to others. The therapist encourages you to talk about this part of your life and about your values and does not immediately turn the discussion back to your inner life.

What to Be Wary of in a Therapist

1. *The therapist discourages all use of moral language.* A good therapist will distinguish between "shoulds" that are moral in nature, such as "I should not put my ex-wife down in front of the children," and those that are based on nonmoral, sometimes oppressive standards, such as "I should finish any job I start," or, "I should look like the fashion models I see in the magazines." In the latter examples, a good therapist is likely to challenge the meaningfulness of the "should" and explore where this injunction came from in your life. In the former case, a good therapist will take the moral dimension of postdivorce parenting very seriously.

2. *The therapist is quick to urge or support cutoffs from other family members.* As I mentioned in chapter 2, a friend of mine was told by her therapist that she was showing an inability to

"grieve" and "move on with her life" when she was not ready to give up on a long-term marriage after her husband's out-of-the-blue announcement, just three weeks prior, that he was having an affair and wanted a separation. Fortunately, my friend fired the therapist. Some therapists are also quick to suggest cutoffs from parents when clients come to understand the abuse they suffered as a child. The therapist may move too soon to recommend that the client write a letter stating, "You abused me, so goodbye," without a full exploration of this decision and its consequences for all concerned, including the client. Often such cutoffs include siblings who were completely innocent but are swept away in a premature, therapist-inspired "family-ectomy." These therapists are like gynecologists who perform unnecessary hysterectomies. I suggest asking a prospective therapist on the phone for his or her philosophy about cutting off contact with family members in cases of abuse.

3. *The therapist sees only negatives in your family or spouse.* A good therapist will demonstrate a realistic but caring attitude toward people close to you. A bad therapist will paint your family members or partner in negative colors only and will interpret your defense of them as denial. This therapist sees others in your life primarily in terms of their poor treatment of you, not as people whom you may care for deeply despite their actions.

4. *The therapist always portrays you as the victim of others, not as someone who also can harm others.* Some therapists work so hard to help abuse victims not blame themselves for the abuse that they lose sight of the here-and-now ways in which the client is hurting or taking advantage of others. A physically abused wife is not responsible for her beatings, but she is responsible for continually telling her son that his father is scum. If your therapist does not challenge behavior you sense is harmful to others, you are not getting good therapy.

5. *The therapist disparages your sense of duty toward others.* When you talk about how hard it is to visit your failing mother in the nursing home, does the therapist ask you to do a cost-benefit analysis—what do you get out of going, and what does it cost you?—without honoring the moral obligation involved? Or when you are struggling to maintain your disabled child in your home, does the therapist continually make the case for your own needs without at the same time supporting your sense of duty to keep your child at home as long as you can? Ditto for community commitments: does the therapist suggest that you are trying to "save the world" to avoid dealing with your personal problems, without acknowledging and supporting the moral imperative you feel to give something back to your community? If so, you are seeing the wrong therapist.

Unfortunately, you may not be able to see many of either the positive qualities or the red flags before getting into therapy. But they can guide your initial inquiries about what the therapist is like and your first talks with the therapist on the phone. When you are already in therapy and your therapist shows behaviors or attitudes that I have classified as warning signs, I encourage you to raise your concerns directly. A caring, brave, and wise therapist will listen carefully to your concerns and work with you to achieve a better balance in the therapy. When I have been pushing too hard for parents to look at the negative side of keeping a child with serious disabilities at home, sometimes they will say, in effect, "Read our lips. We want to find a way to keep our child at home for now." I almost always realign my energies to support their commitment. Good therapists are willing to discuss, and be challenged about, their stance toward moral responsibilities.

My greatest concern about promoting the moral consultation role for therapists is that most of us have not been trained to do it, nor do we have a forum in which to talk about moral and community issues. But there is no going back. We already do provide moral consultation disguised as psychological consultation. I am suggesting that we begin to do it more consciously and explicitly—and hopefully better. Nevertheless, I am still concerned about setting therapists loose without moorings in the moral arena. There are already some therapists out there who feel free to impose their moral judgments on clients—telling couples to stay married, for example. I don't want to expand the number of therapists who see morality in psychotherapy as the straightforward prescription of unambiguous moral standards, instead of a delicate blend of clarifying, exploring, thinking together, and occasionally challenging. And we do not need therapists promoting ill-conceived moral positions that they have never aired and discussed with colleagues. Idiosyncratic moral philosophies that are not subject to dialogue and challenge can be as dangerous in therapy as they are in politics and other settings.

As I mentioned in chapter 1, most practicing therapists are members of a case consultation group in which they discuss difficult clinical cases and get feedback and suggestions. These meetings are often pressed for time, since there are usually more than enough cases to discuss. The result is that most case consultations do not lend themselves to careful evaluation of the therapist's mode of dealing with issues of interpersonal moral responsibility, professional ethics in the changing health care system, and better communities. Strictly clinical concerns swamp other concerns. Graduate school and clinical training settings are better suited to this kind of exploration, but instructors have to make a place for moral and community issues in the curriculum and in supervised internships, not just in the mandatory ethics courses, which often focus mainly on the ethical appropriateness of the therapist's behavior in areas such as confidentiality and informed consent. And training programs rarely pay explicit attention to the development of the character of the trainee.

Therapists need to create groups to educate one another about moral consultation in psychotherapy and about the role of therapists in promoting community well-being. Inspired by the salon movement created by *Utne Reader* magazine, my colleague Patrick Dougherty and I approached an influential magazine for therapists, *Family Therapy Networker*, about the idea of creating a national network of forums or discussion groups for therapists to explore the reenvisioning of psychotherapy as a moral and community-sensitive enterprise. The editor, Richard Simon, immediately liked the idea and offered to sponsor it, first in the Twin Cities and then nationally.

Following is the description we used to invite therapists of all clinical persuasions (not just family therapists) to join the movement. The Minnesota forums began in September 1994, and the National Network forums are being launched in the spring and summer of 1995. Therapists are welcome to use these ideas and materials to develop groups with their own colleagues. Or they can contact *Family Therapy Networker* for assistance at 7705 13th Street, N.W., Washington, DC 20012.

Network Forums for Therapists on Moral, Ethical, and Community Issues

WHAT ARE NETWORK FORUMS?

Network forums are discussion groups of therapists who meet to explore moral, ethical, and community concerns that generally are not addressed in other professional settings.

WHAT KINDS OF ISSUES ARE DISCUSSED?

Although each forum is autonomous and free to pursue its members' interests, the following questions about moral, ethical, and community concerns can be used to open discussion:

1. Can psychotherapy be value-free, or should it even try to be? What is the role of morality in psychotherapy? Where do issues such as justice, honesty, and responsibility to others fit in? How do we deal with moral issues in the lives of our clients without preaching to them, invading their autonomy, or pretending that moral concerns are merely psychological issues in disguise?

2. What virtues must therapists have to practice good therapy? What is the role of character traits such as integrity, truthfulness, caring, and courage? How can therapists exhibit these qualities in the current health care marketplace?

3. What is the role of psychotherapy in promoting the survival and well-being of community? Are we helping clients create psychological cocoons for themselves at the expense of their communities?

4. What should therapists be contributing to our communities beyond our work with specific clients? What values do we "profess" to the larger world, and how can we enact those values?

5. How can the profession and practice of psychotherapy change in a way that is consistent with our values and also responds to the legitimate demands of managed care companies and the government for accountability in the use of fiscal and human resources?

6. In promoting widely available mental health care, how can therapists separate out self-interest from the needs of citizens and consumers? How can therapists maintain their professional integrity as healers in a health care system that is demanding more and more adjustment in therapists' standards of care?

What Is the Spirit of the Forums?

We hope the forums will be supportive and challenging both professionally and personally, that they will be open to a range of ideas and persuasions, and that most discussions will touch on clinical practice, the person of the therapist, and the needs of the larger community. Rather than just critiquing the status quo, we hope forum participants will take the next difficult steps by asking, "How are we part of this problem?" and, "How can we contribute to its solution?"

TRAPS TO AVOID IN CONDUCTING FORUMS

- Duplicating case consultations
- Getting into debates about therapy models
- Losing the focus on moral and ethical issues by reducing everything to pragmatic considerations or legalities
- Losing the focus on community issues (many therapists are more comfortable at the personal and clinical levels)
- Letting professional guild issues predominate
- Blaming other systems and forces in society without also examining our part

HOW WILL THE FORUMS WORK?

Based on the experience of the Minnesota forums, we suggest the following logistics to begin the groups. Once formed, the forums will be autonomous.

- Holding monthly two-hour meetings
- Inviting about fifteen members to join
- Designating someone to host the meetings
- Designating someone to facilitate the discussions
- Designating someone to serve as liaison with the *Family Therapy Networker* forum movement
- Deciding at the first meeting on topics, format, future places to meet, and other logistical issues

Psychotherapy is at a crossroads in the United States at the end of the twentieth century. One road leads to increased medicalization—reducing psychotherapy to a technique for treating narrowly conceived mental disorders when medication is not sufficient—and increased commodification—reducing psychotherapy to a cost item in the health care budget that must be carefully rationed and controlled. If the field takes that road, the argument of this book will be essentially irrelevant and the practice of moral lobotomy in clinical and public discourse will go unchallenged by the community of therapists.

The other road leads to an expansion of psychotherapy beyond its pretenses to being a value-free form of treatment and beyond its love affair with expressive individualism, its preference for technique over character, and its lack of social conscience. There are no maps that clearly show how to take this road. In fact, we will have to build it as we go, in partnership with our clients and our communities. If we build it well, someday it may become the road more traveled.

References

Chapter 1.
Psychotherapy and Moral Responsibility

1. Philip Rieff, *The Triumph of the Therapeutic* (New York: Harper & Row, 1966).
2. Gary R. Vandenbos, Nicholas A. Cummings, and Patrick H. Deleon, "A Century of Psychotherapy: Economic and Environmental Influences," in *History of Psychotherapy: A Century of Change*, ed. Donald K. Freedheim (Washington, DC: American Psychological Association, 1992), pp. 65–102; "Does Psychotherapy Work?" *U.S. News and World Report* (May 24, 1993): 57–64.
3. James Hillman and Michael Ventura, *We've Had a Hundred Years of Psychotherapy—and the World's Getting Worse* (San Francisco: Harper San Francisco, 1992).
4. Peter Marks, "Psychologist Is Pressured on Views by Judge in Allen Custody Case," *New York Times*, April 27, 1993.
5. Charles J. Sykes, *A Nation of Victims* (New York: St. Martin's Press, 1992).
6. Alasdair MacIntyre, *After Virtue* (South Bend, IN: University of Notre Dame Press, 1984); Jurgen Habermas, "Law as Medium and Law as Institution," in *Dilemmas of Law in the Welfare State*, ed. G. Teubner (New York: Walter de Gruyter, 1986); Rieff, *Triumph of the Therapeutic*; Philip Rieff, *Freud: The Mind of the Moralist* (Garden City, NY: Anchor Books, 1961); Robert N. Bellah, Richard Madsen,

William M. Sullivan, Ann Swidler, and Steven M. Tipton, *Habits of the Heart: Individualism and Commitment in American Life* (Berkeley: University of California Press, 1985), and *The Good Society* (New York: Knopf, 1991); Christopher Lasch, *The Culture of Narcissism* (New York: Warner Books, 1979); Michael Lerner, *Surplus Powerlessness: The Psychodynamics of Everyday Life—And the Psychology of Individual and Social Transformation* (Atlantic Highland, NJ: Humanities Press International, 1991); Michael A. Wallach and Lise Wallach, *Psychology's Sanction for Selfishness: The Error of Egoism in Theory and Therapy* (San Francisco: W. H. Freeman, 1983).

7. For a well-written article on the managed care crisis for therapists, see Mary Sykes Wylie, "Endangered Species: Is Private Practice Becoming an Oxymoron?" *Family Therapy Networker* 18 (March–April 1994): 20–33.

8. Ellen Goodman, "Good, Bad, and Psychobabble," *Minneapolis–St. Paul Star Tribune*, April 6, 1993.

9. Rieff, *Freud*, p. 391.

10. Rieff, *Triumph of the Therapeutic*, p. 5; see also Thomas Szasz, *The Myth of Psychotherapy*, 2d ed. (Syracuse, NY: Syracuse University Press, 1988).

11. The major exception to the pattern of avoiding moral issues in psychotherapy is the psychiatrist and family therapist Ivan Boszormenyi-Nagy, who made intergenerational ethics the core of his theory and his therapy. See Ivan Boszormenyi-Nagy, *Foundations of Contextual Therapy* (New York: Brunner/Mazel, 1987). Outside of psychotherapy, Erik Erikson was a prominent theorist of human development with a strong ethical emphasis, particularly on the theme of generativity toward the next generation. For a discussion of this theme in Erikson's work, see John Snarey, *How Fathers Care for the Next Generation: A Four-Decade Study* (Cambridge, MA: Harvard University Press, 1993).

12. Fritz Perls, *Gestalt Therapy Verbatim* (Lafayette, CA: Real People Press, 1969), p. 4.

13. Gail Sheehy, *Passages: Predictable Crises of Adult Life* (New York: Bantam Books, 1976), pp. 364, 513.

14. See, for example, Amitai Etzioni, *The Spirit of Community: Rights, Responsibilities, and the Communitarian Agenda* (New York: Crown, 1993); Stephen L. Carter, *The Culture of Disbelief: How American Law and Politics Trivialize Religious Devotion* (New York: Basic Books, 1993); Jean Bethke Elshtain, "The Family and Civic Life," in

Rebuilding the Nest: A New Commitment to the American Family, ed. David Blankenhorn, Steven Bayme, and Jean Bethke Elshtain (Milwaukee, WI: Family Service America, 1990), pp. 119–32; Mary Ann Glendon, *Abortion and Divorce in Western Law* (Cambridge, MA: Harvard University Press, 1987).

15. James Q. Wilson, *The Moral Sense* (New York: Free Press, 1993), p. 16.

16. Rollo May, foreword to Freedheim, *History of Psychotherapy*, p. xxv.

17. For a discussion of how autonomous individualism emerged as a male prerogative in American culture, see Elizabeth Fox-Genovese, *Feminism Without Illusions: A Critique of Individualism* (Chapel Hill: University of North Carolina Press, 1991). Fox-Genovese's call for feminism to transcend its own individualistic roots has been criticized by some feminists as premature, given the unfinished work in gaining individual rights for women; see Ruth Rosen's review of Fox-Genovese's book in *Women's Review of Books* 8, no. 2 (September 1991): 20. See Carol Gilligan, *In a Different Voice: Psychological Theory and Women's Development* (Cambridge, MA: Harvard University Press, 1982).

18. Rachel Hare-Mustin, "A Feminist Approach to Family Therapy," *Family Process* 17 (1978): 181–94; Judith Worell and Pam Remer, *Feminist Perspectives in Therapy* (New York: John Wiley, 1992); Nancy Boyd-Franklin, *Black Families in Therapy* (New York: Guilford Press, 1989).

19. Robert Jay Lifton, *The Life of the Self: Toward a New Psychology* (New York: Basic Books, 1983), p. 152.

20. See Philip Cushman, "Psychotherapy to 1992: A Historically Situated Interpretation," in Freedheim, *History of Psychotherapy*, pp. 21–64; Edward E. Sampson, "The Debate on Individualism: Indigenous Psychologies of the Individual and Their Role in Personal and Societal Functioning," *American Psychologist* 43 (1988): 15–22.

21. Allen E. Bergin, "Psychotherapy and Religious Values," *Journal of Consulting and Clinical Psychology* 48 (1980): 95–105; Carter, *Culture of Disbelief.*

22. See Mary W. Nicholas, *The Mystery of Goodness and the Positive Moral Consequences of Psychotherapy* (New York: Norton, 1994); August G. Lageman, *The Moral Dimensions of Marriage and Family Therapy* (Lanham, MD: University Press of America, 1993); M. Scott Peck, *The Road Less Traveled* (New York: Simon & Schuster, 1978); Perry London, *The Modes and Morals of Psychotherapy*, 2d ed. (Washington,

DC: Hemisphere, 1986); Joseph Margolis, *Psychotherapy and Morality: A Study of Two Concepts* (New York: Random House, 1966); Jeremy Holmes and Richard Lindley, *The Values of Psychotherapy* (New York: Oxford University Press, 1989); Neal O. Weiner, *The Harmony of the Soul: Mental Health and Moral Virtue Reconsidered* (Albany: State University of New York Press, 1993); William J. Doherty and Pauline G. Boss, "Values and Ethics in Family Therapy," in *The Handbook of Family Therapy*, 2d ed. (New York: Brunner/Mazel, 1991), pp. 606–37; James W. Maddock, "Ecology, Ethics, and Responsibility in Family Therapy," *Family Relations* 42 (1993): 116–23.

23. William J. Doherty and Macaran A. Baird, *Family Therapy and Family Medicine* (New York: Guilford Press, 1983); Susan H. McDaniel, Jeri Hepworth, and William J. Doherty, *Medical Family Therapy* (New York: Basic Books, 1992).

24. See Thomas Kitwood, *Concern for Others: A New Psychology of Conscience and Morality* (New York: Routledge, 1990); and Nicholas, *The Mystery of Goodness*.

25. Alan Wolfe, *Whose Keeper? Social Science and Moral Obligation* (Berkeley: University of California Press, 1989), pp. 214–15.

26. Ibid., p. 211.

Chapter 2. Commitment

1. See David B. Waters and Edith C. Lawrence, *Competence, Courage, and Change: An Approach to Family Therapy* (New York: Norton, 1993), pp. 111–14.

2. For an exception, see Ivan Boszormenyi-Nagy, *Foundations of Contextual Therapy* (New York: Brunner/Mazel, 1987).

3. See Robert N. Bellah, Richard Madsen, William M. Sullivan, Ann Swidler, and Steven M. Tipton, *Habits of the Heart: Individualism and Commitment in American Life* (Berkeley: University of California Press, 1985), pp. 93–97.

4. See James Q. Wilson, *The Moral Sense* (New York: Free Press, 1993), p. 2; Alan Wolfe, *Whose Keeper? Social Science and Moral Obligation* (Berkeley: University of California Press, 1989), p. 211.

5. Diane Vaughan, *Uncoupling: How Relationships Come Apart* (New York: Oxford University Press, 1986).

6. See a series of articles on this theme in *Family Therapy Networker* 18 (May–June 1994).

7. In a book arguing for the primacy of loyalty or commitment in human relationships, George Fletcher also makes the point that commitment can become a moral trap if there are no limits beyond which it is sensible to go in sustaining a relationship, and that the threat of "exit" can be a legitimate and powerful medium for correcting what is wrong. See George P. Fletcher, *Loyalty: An Essay on the Morality of Relationships* (New York: Oxford University Press, 1993). On the issue of the effects of marital conflict on children, see Robert E. Emery, *Marriage, Divorce, and Children's Adjustment* (Newbury Park, CA: Sage, 1988).

8. Wolfe, *Whose Keeper*, pp. 216, 221.

9. Ibid., p. 127.

10. Wilson, *The Moral Sense*, pp. 2, 250.

11. See Lawrence Kohlberg, *The Meaning and Measurement of Moral Development* (Worcester, MA: Clark University Press, 1991); John Rawls, *A Theory of Justice* (New York: Oxford University Press, 1972).

12. Carol Gilligan, *In a Different Voice: Psychological Theory and Women's Development* (Cambridge, MA: Harvard University Press, 1982).

13. George Herbert Mead, *On Social Psychology: Selected Papers*, ed. Anselm Strauss (Chicago: University of Chicago Press, 1956); Peter Berger and Thomas Luckmann, *The Social Construction of Reality* (New York: Doubleday, 1966); Herbert Blumer, *Symbolic-Interactionism: Perspective and Method* (Englewood Cliffs, NJ: Prentice-Hall, 1969).

14. Morality as a form of discourse is the major theme of Richard A. Shweder's anthropological work; see chapter 5 in *Thinking Through Cultures* (Cambridge, MA: Harvard University Press, 1991). Following Alasdair MacIntyre, the philosopher Mark Johnson views narrative, or storytelling—the structures of which are inherited from our traditions—as the heart of moral explanation. See Mark Johnson, *Moral Imagination* (Chicago: University of Chicago Press, 1993), pp. 179–84.

15. Wilson, *The Moral Sense*, pp. ix, xii.

16. See Howard Clinebell, *Basic Types of Pastoral Care and Counseling* (Nashville, TN: Abingdon Press, 1984), ch. 8.

Chapter 3. Justice

1. See Benina Berger Gould and Donna Hilleboe DeMuth, *The Global Family Therapist: Integrating the Personal, Professional, and Political* (Boston: Allyn & Bacon, 1994); Michael Lerner, *Surplus Powerlessness:*

The Psychodynamics of Everyday Life—And the Psychology of Individual and Social Transformation (Atlantic Highland, NJ: Humanities Press International, 1991).

2. Ivan Boszormenyi-Nagy and Barbara R. Krasner, *Between Give and Take: A Clinical Guide to Contextual Therapy* (New York: Brunner/Mazel, 1986); Ivan Boszormenyi-Nagy, *Foundations of Contextual Therapy* (New York: Brunner/Mazel, 1987).

3. For exceptions, see Boszormenyi-Nagy and Krasner, *Between Give and Take*; and Mary W. Nicholas, *The Mystery of Goodness and the Positive Moral Consequences of Psychotherapy* (New York: Norton, 1994).

4. See Marianne Walters, Betty Carter, Peggy Papp, and Olga Silverstein, *The Invisible Web: Gender Patterns in Family Relationships* (New York: Guilford Press, 1988); Monica McGoldrick, Carol M. Anderson, and Froma Walsh, eds., *Women in Families: A Framework for Family Therapy* (New York: Norton, 1989).

5. Carol Gilligan, Janie Victoria Ward, and Jill McLean Taylor, eds., *Mapping the Moral Domain* (Cambridge, MA: Harvard University Press, 1988); Mary Jeanne Larrabee, ed., *An Ethic of Care: Feminist and Interdisciplinary Perspectives* (New York: Routledge, 1993).

Chapter 4. Truthfulness

1. Sissela Bok, *Lying: Moral Choice in Public and Private Life* (New York: Vintage Books, 1979).

2. See, for example, Sigmund Freud, *New Introductory Lectures on Psychoanalysis*, tr. James Strachey (1935; New York: Norton, 1965); Carl R. Rogers, *Client-Centered Therapy* (Boston: Houghton Mifflin, 1965).

3. See, for example, Albert Ellis and Russell Grieger, *Handbook of Rational-Emotive Therapy* (New York: Springer, 1977); Wendy Dryden and William L. Golden, eds., *Cognitive-Behavioral Approaches to Psychotherapy* (New York: Harper & Row, 1987).

4. For a book on the effect of secrets and deception on families, written for therapists, see Evan Imber-Black, ed., *Secrets in Families and Family Therapy* (New York: Norton, 1993). Harriet G. Lerner's *The Dance of Deception* (New York: HarperCollins, 1993) is a book for lay readers and professionals on deception and truth-telling in women's lives.

5. Ivan Boszormenyi-Nagy, *Foundations of Contextual Therapy* (New York: Brunner/Mazel, 1987).

6. Bok, *Lying*, p. 33 (Bok's emphasis).
7. Ibid., p. 16.
8. Ibid., pp. 158–59.
9. Rachel Hare-Mustin, "Discourses in the Mirrored Room: A Postmodern Analysis of Therapy," *Family Process* 33 (1994): 19–35.
10. Charles Taylor, *The Ethics of Authenticity* (Cambridge, MA: Harvard University Press, 1992).
11. Ibid., p. 14.
12. Ibid., p. 4.
13. Ibid., pp. 15, 74.
14. Ibid., pp. 72–73.
15. Bok, *Lying*, pp. 60–76.
16. See William J. Doherty and Pauline G. Boss, "Values and Ethics in Family Therapy," in *The Handbook of Family Therapy*, 2d ed. (New York: Brunner/Mazel, 1991), pp. 606–37.

Chapter 5. Community

1. Susan H. McDaniel, Jeri Hepworth, and William J. Doherty, *Medical Family Therapy* (New York: Basic Books, 1992).
2. See Sylvia Staub and Paul Green, eds., *Psychology and Social Responsibility* (New York: New York University Press, 1992); Evan Imber-Black, *Families and Larger Systems* (New York: Guilford Press, 1988); Marsha Pravder Mirkin, ed., *The Social and Political Contexts of Family Therapy* (Needham, MA: Allyn & Bacon, 1990); Nancy Boyd-Franklin, *Black Families in Therapy* (New York: Guilford Press, 1989). Even M. Scott Peck, the widely read self-help author, has moved in recent years in the direction of emphasizing the individual within a community context; see M. Scott Peck, *The Different Drum: Community-Making and Peace* (New York: Simon & Schuster, 1992). On the same theme as it concerns physician-patient relationships, see Howard Waitzkin, *The Politics of Medical Encounters* (New Haven, CT: Yale University Press, 1991).
3. See Anderson J. Franklin, "The Invisibility Syndrome," *Family Therapy Networker* 17 (July–August 1993): 32–39; Michael Lerner, *Surplus Powerlessness: The Psychodynamics of Everyday Life—And the Psychology of Individual and Social Transformation* (Atlantic Highland, NJ: Humanities Press International, 1991), ch. 16.
4. In addition to the feminist books cited previously, see Judith Worell

and Pam Remer, *Feminist Perspectives in Therapy* (New York: John Wiley, 1992); Laura S. Brown and Maria P. P. Root, eds., *Diversity and Complexity in Feminist Therapy* (New York: Harrington Park Press, 1990); Marsha Pravder Mirkin, ed., *Women in Context: Toward a Feminist Reconstruction of Psychotherapy* (New York: Guilford Press, 1994).

5. Franklin, "Invisibility Syndrome," pp. 32–39. See also the political theorist William A. Galston, who discusses the importance of a balance between "both sides of the moral equation": the influence of social context on behavior and the "necessary presumption of human freedom [which] must not be replaced with the debasing psychology of victimization." William A. Galston, *Liberal Purposes: Goods, Virtues, and Diversity in the Liberal State* (New York: Cambridge University Press, 1991), p. 289.

6. Robert N. Bellah, Richard Madsen, William M. Sullivan, Ann Swidler, and Steven M. Tipton, *The Good Society* (New York: Knopf, 1991), p. 6.

7. See Alan Wolfe, *Whose Keeper? Social Science and Moral Obligation* (Berkeley: University of California Press, 1989); Jurgen Habermas, "Law as Medium and Law as Institution," in *Dilemmas of Law in the Welfare State*, ed. G. Teubner (New York: Walter de Gruyter, 1986).

8. For expositions of the civil society, see Wolfe, *Whose Keeper*, pp. 13–19; Adam B. Seligman, *The Idea of Civil Society* (New York: Free Press, 1992).

9. Wolfe, *Whose Keeper*, pp. 18–19.

10. Ibid., p. 12.

11. Cross-National Collaborative Group, "The Changing Rate of Major Depression: Cross-National Comparisons," *Journal of the American Medical Association* 268 (1992): 3098–3105.

12. Emile Durkheim, *Suicide*, tr. J. A. Spaulding and G. Simpson (Glencoe, IL: Free Press, 1951).

13. See the discussion of individual self-interest, community, and citizenship in Robert N. Bellah, Richard Madsen, William M. Sullivan, Ann Swidler, and Steven M. Tipton, *Habits of the Heart: Individualism and Commitment in American Life* (Berkeley: University of California Press, 1985), pp. 152–218.

14. Wolfe, *Whose Keeper*, p. 18. For a feminist-inspired discussion of the dangers of romanticizing traditional communities, see Marilyn Friedman, "Feminism and Modern Friendship: Dislocating the Community," in *Communitarianism and Individualism*, ed. Shlomo

Avineri and Avner De-Shalit (New York: Oxford University Press, 1992), pp. 101–19.

15. Mary W. Nicholas, *The Mystery of Goodness and the Positive Moral Consequences of Psychotherapy* (New York: Norton, 1994).

16. Andrew Samuels, *The Political Psyche* (New York: Routledge, 1993).

17. James Hillman and Michael Ventura, *We've Had a Hundred Years of Psychotherapy—and the World's Getting Worse* (San Francisco: Harper San Francisco, 1992), p. 40.

18. Anne Colby and William Damon, *Some Do Care: Contemporary Lives of Moral Commitment* (New York: Free Press, 1992). In the best-selling book *Listening to Prozac* (New York: Penguin Books, 1993), Peter D. Kramer voices concerns that psychopharmacologic medications such as Prozac may numb moral sensibilities by taking away the compulsive quality of urgent moral outrage and action (pp. 291–300).

19. Taylor, *The Ethics of Authenticity* (Cambridge, MA: Harvard University Press, 1992), p. 9; Alexis de Tocqueville, *Democracy in America*, Vol. 2 (New York: Vintage Books, 1990), pp. 316–30.

20. Ibid., pp. 40–41 (Taylor's emphasis).

21. Richard Sherman, "Mental Health Practice in a Global Context," in Staub and Green, *Psychology and Social Responsibility*, pp. 221–34.

22. Dusty Miller, *Women Who Hurt Themselves* (New York: Basic Books, 1994), pp. 199–200; Judith Lewis Herman, *Trauma and Recovery* (New York: Basic Books, 1992), pp. 70–73.

23. See Amitai Etzioni, *The Spirit of Community: Rights, Responsibilities, and the Communitarian Agenda* (New York: Crown, 1993); Avineri and De-Shalit, *Communitarianism and Individualism*; Daniel Bell, *Communitarianism and Its Critics* (New York: Oxford University Press, 1993).

Chapter 6. Caring

1. See John W. Chapman and William A. Galston, eds., *Virtue* (New York: New York University Press, 1992); Alasdair MacIntyre, *After Virtue* (South Bend, IN: University of Notre Dame Press, 1984).

2. MacIntyre, *After Virtue*; Edmund D. Pellegrino and David C. Thomasma, *The Virtues in Medical Practice* (New York: Oxford University Press, 1993); August G. Lageman, *The Moral Dimension of Marriage and Family Therapy* (Lanham, MD: University Press of America, 1993); Mary W. Nicholas, *The Mystery of Goodness and the Positive Moral Consequences of Psychotherapy* (New York: Norton,

1994); Michael A. Slote, *From Morality to Virtue* (New York: Oxford University Press, 1992).

3. Pellegrino and Thomasma, *The Virtues in Medical Practice*, pp. 51–61.

4. MacIntyre, *After Virtue*, ch. 13.

5. Pellegrino and Thomasma, *The Virtues in Medical Practice*, p. xii.

6. See Charles H. Patterson, *The Therapeutic Relationship* (Monterey, CA: Brooks/Cole, 1985).

7. Viktor E. Frankl, *The Will to Meaning* (New York: World, 1969), p. 8.

8. Carl R. Rogers, *Client-Centered Therapy* (Boston: Houghton Mifflin, 1965).

9. Seymour Sarason, *Caring and Compassion in Clinical Practice* (San Francisco: Jossey-Bass, 1985).

10. Ibid., p. 7.

11. Ibid., pp. 186–204.

12. Nel Noddings, *Caring: A Feminine Approach to Ethics and Moral Education* (Berkeley: University of California Press, 1984).

13. Ibid., p. 5.

14. Ibid., p. 10.

15. Yvonne Stolk and Amaryll J. Perlesz, "Do Better Trainees Make Worse Family Therapists? A Followup Study of Client Families," *Family Process* 29 (1990): 45–58.

16. Eve Lipchik, "The Rush to Be Brief," *Family Therapy Networker* 18 (March–April 1994): 34–39.

17. Noddings, *Caring*, p. 105.

18. Franklin, "Invisibility Syndrome," pp. 32–39.

19. See Marilyn R. Peterson, *At Personal Risk: Boundary Violations in Professional-Client Relationships* (New York: Norton, 1992).

20. Noddings, *Caring*, pp. 98–103.

21. Ibid., pp. 23–26.

22. Sarason, *Caring and Compassion in Clinical Practice*, pp. 132–57.

Chapter 7. Courage

1. David B. Waters and Edith C. Lawrence, *Competence, Courage, and Change: An Approach to Family Therapy* (New York: Norton, 1993).

2. Ibid., p. 114.

3. Ibid.

4. The courage of honest self-awareness as a way to avoid exploiting clients is well documented in Marilyn R. Peterson, *At Personal Risk:*

Boundary Violations in Professional-Client Relationships (New York: Norton, 1992).

Chapter 8. Prudence

1. See Michael D. Yapko, *Suggestions of Abuse: True and False Memories of Childhood Sexual Trauma* (New York: Simon & Schuster, 1994).
2. See Elizabeth F. Loftus, "The Reality of Repressed Memories," *American Psychologist* 48 (1993): 518–37.
3. See Mary Sykes Wylie, "The Shadow of a Doubt" *Family Therapy Networker* 17 (September–October 1993): 18–29, 70, 73.
4. See Kathleen A. Kendall-Tackett, Linda Meyer Williams, and David Finkelhor, "Impact of Sexual Abuse on Children: A Review and Synthesis of Recent Empirical Studies," *Psychological Bulletin* 113 (1993): 164–80.
5. See Lawrence Wright, *Remembering Satan* (New York: Knopf, 1994).
6. Ibid.

INDEX